Scenic Spots

SCENIC

Chinese Tourism, the State,

A CHINA PROGRAM BOOK

UNIVERSITY OF WASHINGTON PRESS

SPOTS

and Cultural Authority

PÁL NYÍRI

Seattle and London

THIS PUBLICATION WAS SUPPORTED IN PART BY THE CHINA STUDIES
PROGRAM, A DIVISION OF THE HENRY M. JACKSON SCHOOL OF
INTERNATIONAL STUDIES AT THE UNIVERSITY OF WASHINGTON.

ADDITIONAL SUPPORT WAS PROVIDED BY THE DIVISION OF SOCIETY,
CULTURE, MEDIA AND PHILOSOPHY, MACQUARIE UNIVERSITY

University of Washington Press
P.O. Box 50096, Seattle, WA 98145 U.S.A.
www.washington.edu/uwpress

Library of Congress Cataloging-in-Publication Data
can be found at the back of this book.

The paper used in this publication is acid-free and 90 percent
recycled from at least 50 percent post-consumer waste. It meets the
minimum requirements of American National Standard for Information Sciences—Permanence of Paper for Printed Library
Materials, ANSI z39.48–1984.

TO JOANA BREIDENBACH, FELLOW TRAVELER

CONTENTS

PREFACE

Dean MacCannell started *The Tourist*—the first and, to this day, the most influential, scholarly study of tourism—by stating that "'the tourist' is one of the best models available for modern-man-in-general" (MacCannell 1976:1). Indeed, both "the traveler" and "the tourist"—not to be confused or conflated—have long been important metaphors for the (post-) modern individual. But what these notions stand for—most often an individual in restless pursuit of knowledge or pleasure and/or escaping every-day alienation—in both this general metaphoric discourse and in the work of MacCannell and numerous other students of tourism after him is actu-ally not "modern-man-in-general," but rather an embodiment of modernity *in the West*, predicated on the free market and liberal democracy. In most social studies of tourism (which generally presume to operate on universal theo-retical claims), the non-Western subject can only be the "touree" who must cope with the consequences of this product of Western modernity (Alneng 2002). Despite sustained critiques by feminist scholars, this equation between tourism and the West remains pervasive, a fact that becomes apparent when one goes through programs of conferences on tourism and even recent work produced by non-Western scholars (e.g., Yamashita 2003).

Yet organized, commercialized mass tourism—a post–World War II development now labeled the biggest business in the world, with revenues of $463 billion in 2001, according to the World Tourism Organization

(WTO, http://www.world-tourism.org)—is spreading to vast populations that had not known it previously. This has potentially momentous consequences both for subjectivities in the societies in which tourism is emerging and for the countries that become exporters of leisure to newly mobile non-Western populations, whose ideas of leisure may be different from those in the West. Understanding the tourist practices of these populations may force us to revise our ideas of "modern-man-in-general."

MacCannell, an American sociologist influenced by European structural anthropology, was ahead of his time both in his method, an attempt to bridge the study of social behavior with the study of texts, and in his subject, travel, which stayed firmly on the fringe of social inquiry until James Clifford's work nearly two decades later. Although MacCannell may be the urtext of "tourism studies," he has remained marginal to mainstream social studies. But meanwhile, following Clifford's and George Marcus's *Writing Culture* and the "scapes" and "flows" focus of the nineties, multi-sited ethnographies have become common, and the barriers between ethnography-based anthropology and text-based cultural studies are gradually being dismantled, though not without a degree of acrimony. In the introduction to *The Tourist*, MacCannell wrote: "I never entertained the notion that the old one-man–one-culture approach to ethnography could be adapted to the study of modern social structure. . . . So I undertook to follow tourists, sometimes joining their groups, sometimes watching them from afar through writings by, for and about them." Today, the synthetic approach of combining ethnographic fieldwork with a historically embedded study of such a highly vernacular form of text as promotional brochures for tourists may require less justification than it did thirty years ago.

This book is about the construction of the tourist and the tourist site in the People's Republic of China. It takes as its starting point the idea that understanding why Chinese tourists pursue certain kinds of experiences and what they make of them—what, for instance, lies behind an elderly former soldier's disappointed dismissal of Berlin as "less modern than even Hangzhou," a provincial capital—requires investigating the construct of the tourist in China's burgeoning tourism industry and understanding the relationship that construct posits between the tourist and the object of tourism, the tourist site. Twenty years ago, there was hardly any commercial tourism in China. Today, Chinese tourism has been created anew. Certain places have been made into tourist sites; others have not. What is it, then, that makes a Chinese tourist site for its producers—state and market actors—and for its consumers? Who has cultural authority over the tourist site and why? These questions relate quite closely to the literature on the history of leisure in modern Europe and America. Like this literature, they ultimately ask why the formation of modernity—in this case, Chinese modernity—has taken the particular path it has. In contrast, they have a rather more remote relationship to the bulk of research on contemporary tourism development, which—particularly when it comes to places outside the West—is concerned chiefly with the economic, environmental, and social change tourism brings to its destinations.

After a review of the emergence of commercial tourism in "reform-era" China, the opening chapter analyses contemporary promotional brochures published by tourism authorities and travel agencies in mainland China, demonstrating their perception of tourism as the consumption of "scenic spots" (*jingdian*), bounded and controlled zones. "Development" and commodification are explicit in these depictions. I trace the representations of scenic spots, which reject the "romantic gaze" and fear of commodification that continue to dominate the Western discourse of tourism, to the history of pre-modern representations of gentry travel in China, which is firmly embedded in the Chinese cultural canon.

The second chapter reports on fieldwork in 2002–03 at two popular Chinese tourist sites—one historically known, Mount Emei, and one newly developed, Jiuzhaigou—and shows how tour guides and tourists frame the consumption of the scenic spot. To define the constitutive features of the scenic spot, I compare Jiuzhaigou to a nearby town, Songpan, which is not a scenic spot for Chinese tourists but is popular with Western backpackers.

The third chapter argues that the revival of pre-modern representations of scenic spots and the maintenance of hegemonic cultural authority over them has been made possible by the absence of the distinctly modern, romantic, exploratory, and self-bettering discourses of tourism that emerged in the West after the Enlightenment. In late socialist China, the notion of the scenic spot has been appropriated by the state's nation-building project and has become hegemonic in the tourism market. Much recent literature on tourism is critical of its portrayal as a homogenizing force and points out the potential of tourist practices to subvert the intent of the producers of tourist sites. Yet in China, to a large degree, the hegemonic representation of scenic spots and of tourism by the state-market matrix defines proper tourist behavior as well as how the sites are read by mainstream tourists. Although the emergence of alternative constructs of tourism suggests possible challenges to this canon, the Chinese construction of the tourist site may be useful for understanding the mechanisms by which the Chinese state has so successfully continued to resist challenges to its authority to represent and interpret Chinese culture.

The concluding chapter considers the increasingly widespread encounters between Chinese tourists and Western tourist landscapes. How do Chinese tourists deal with the far less canonized meanings of sites they encounter outside China? How are alternative sources of authority established over the interpretation of such sites? These questions are particularly important because of the central role of cross-border mobility in discourses of what it means to be Chinese in the modern world. These discourses have so far largely interpreted such mobility as migration, driven by the purpose of capital accumulation, but they are likely to shift as the purpose of movement expands to a consumption-oriented framework of travel as leisure.

I am deeply indebted to Joana Breidenbach, who participated in both the fieldwork and the analysis relating to this research, for her continuous help and inspiration. Fieldwork for this book was carried out with support from the Humanities Center, Central European University. The manuscript, written while on a fellowship at the Wissenschaftskolleg zu Berlin, benefited from discussions with Catherine Vance Yeh—to whom I am especially thankful for reading and commenting on an early version—as well as with Xin Liu, Robert P. Weller, Eileen R. Walsh, and the Kolleg's fellows, particularly Rudolf G. Wagner, Ramie Targoff, Stephen Greenblatt, Peter Hall, Ines G. Zupanov, Rossitza Guentcheva, Heike Paul, Cui Zhiyuan, and Ulrich Herbert. I also thank Rudolf Wagner, Diana Yeh, Jacques Lévy, Serguei Alex. Oushakine, Magdalena Nowicka, and Irina Sandomirskaja for pointing me to numerous helpful writings in the course of the work, and the staff of the Wissenschaftskolleg zu Berlin and Cordula Gumbrecht of the Berlin State Library-Prussian Cultural Fund for providing them. Finally, I thank the two anonymous reviewers for the University of Washington Press for their helpful critique.

Scenic Spots

1

WHAT'S IN A SITE?

The Making of "Scenic Spots"

The cover of the March 1982 issue of *Tourist* (Lüyou), one of China's newly launched travel magazines, shows the tourist as Westerner. Unlike the Soviet Union, where a form of what we might call wilderness tourism was valorized as contributing to the physical and moral fitness of the Soviet person, Maoist China saw tourism as an element of bourgeois lifestyle and therefore, in principle, taboo (Zhang Guangrui 2003:15). Tourism was also effectively absent from people's everyday lives and vocabularies. A peculiar exception to this was the "pilgrimages" of Red Guards to revolutionary sites during the Cultural Revolution. These sites, classified in a state-approved list with a hierarchy of three levels, constituted a canonized set that Rudolf Wagner (1992:380–86) called "the religious geography of new China."

In the decades since 1978—officially known as the era of "reform and opening"—rising incomes and the appearance of a consumer class with a state-sanctioned concept of a holiday have made possible the emergence of a Chinese tourism, slow at first but very rapid in the last decade. This development has been closely tied to state policies.

After Mao's death, the ideological stigma of tourism began to fade as the Chinese government opened the country to incoming tourism as a way to earn foreign currency. But the view of tourism as first and foremost a modern Western practice (fig. 1) persisted into the early 1990s. Thus an article

3

FIG. 1. *The Westerner as the tourist, 1982. Cover of* Tourist *(Beijing), March 1982. Berlin State Library-Prussian Cultural Fund.*

entitled "China's Tourism Business in '90: Looking Back and Looking Ahead," published in the then five-year-old professional journal *Tourism Tribune* (Lüyou xuekan), talks exclusively about incoming tourism (National Tourism Administration 1991). Most of the incoming tourists were ethnic Chinese from Hong Kong, Taiwan, and Southeast Asia rather than "real

Westerners" (Zhang Guangrui 2003:16). (The primary target of tourism development was reflected in the fact that the state-owned China Travel Service was subordinated to the Overseas Chinese Affairs Bureau.) This period witnessed the proliferation of Chinese translations of English-language literature on tourism management,[1] as officials and managers in charge of tourism argued for a "scientific" approach to developing China's "tourism product" (e.g., Li Hairui 1991; Zhang Yongxian 1991; Xiao Tihui 1991). Although they increasingly acknowledged the appearance of domestic tourists (e.g., Jing 1991), they still ignored them in these discussions or relegated them to a secondary position, as did the official of the Anhui Province Tourism Bureau who proposed that international tourists should be "the main consumer base" of "national- and provincial-level key tourist products," while domestic tourists "lead" the development of ordinary products "below provincial level" (Zhang Yongxian 1991:30).

The Emergence of Chinese Tourism

The development of domestic tourism is variously reported to have first appeared on the central government's agenda in a speech by Secretary-General Hu Yaobang in 1985 (Wei et al. 1999:145) or by Prime Minister Li Peng in 1991. In any case, although the National Tourism Administration created a domestic travel department in 1985, the first high-level document on domestic tourism development was a plan approved by the State Council in 1993 (ibid.). By the late 1990s, thanks to a combination of growing incomes and a series of new policies, it became a mass phenomenon. After the introduction of the five-day workweek in 1995, the National Tourism Administration declared 1996 the Year of Leisure and Vacation (Honggen Xiao 2003:273) as part of the government's "leisure culture campaign" (Jing Wang 2001:39), and, in 1997, it made developing domestic tourism a priority in its policy for the first time (Qian 2003:148). Finally, in 1998, when general domestic consumption slackened and threatened economic growth, the Central Committee of the Chinese Communist Party decided to promote tourism as a remedy (Wei et al. 1999:4). To facilitate it, the government in 1999 raised the number of holidays from eight to ten days, creating three weeks off: one each around the 1 October and 1 May state holidays and the traditional lunar Spring Festival. Additionally, private companies often provide their employees with another week of collective holidays, which, if the company is not very large, they will frequently spend traveling together.

The introduction of the three week-long holidays resulted in a revolution in Chinese leisure that was underscored by a series of meetings on domestic tourism organized by the national and provincial Tourism Administrations, at which Party and government leaders pledged their support for developing the sector and offered some incentives for investing in it (Wei et al. 1999:147). The holiday periods, which came to be known as "golden weeks," became times for the urban consumer class to travel. During the 1999 Spring Festival period, six hundred thousand Shanghainese left the city to travel.

All of a sudden, tourism gained prominence as a lifestyle attribute of the higher-income urban population and began spreading to an increasingly large part of Chinese society. China is still far from being a "leisure society"— one in which expectations of leisure shape definitions of work (MacCannell 1976:1–37; Koshar 2002:15)—and the Westerner's familiar complaint, "I really need a holiday!" would sound strange in a country where there is little conceptual separation between working time and leisure time and little institutionalization of times when one should not work. But the concept of holiday or vacation (*dujia*) has established itself strongly enough in China's consumer culture that younger people have taken to traveling even during the Spring Festival, a time traditionally spent with relatives in one's ancestral village. It is important to note that this change took place with the active (both administrative and "pedagogical") participation of the state. While the crucial 1998 decision to promote tourism was justified in terms of economic development (Wei et al. 1999:4), as Jing Wang points out, it coincided with the appearance of the term "leisure culture" (*xiuxian wenhua*) in the government's "civilization campaigns" as one of the attributes of the "modern and civilized citizen/burgher [*shimin*]" (Jing Wang 2001:39–41).[2]

During the "golden week" between 1 and 7 October 2002, Chinese citizens purchased ninety million tickets to China's "tourist zones," 12 percent more than during the same period in the previous year and breaking the record set in May.[3] Apart from giving us an idea of growth, however, the nature of these data also reflects the perception of tourism in China. Unlike the West, where hotel nights are the most common tourism indicator, in China tourism authorities use ticket-sales data from tourist sites or "scenic spots," recognized and classified by the state, to gauge the volume of domestic tourism.[4] As far as the state and the tourism business are concerned, the map of China consists of a network of scenic spots ranging from imperial palaces and revolutionary memorials to nature reserves. An official of the National Tourism Administration has labeled tourism "the spot business" (Li Hairui 1991).

Scenic spots even have an association: the Scenic Spots Association of China (Zhongguo Fengjing Mingshengqu Xiehui). By contrast, domestic travel to other locations, or travel that does not engage with these state-sanctioned sites, falls outside tourism statistics. Thus, tourism in China is understood by its managers as the consumption of bounded and controlled zones.

Scenic Spots: A Cultural History

The most frequent term for scenic spot is *jingdian*, often preceded by the adjective *lüyou* (travel/tourist), while more formal expressions used are *fengjingqu* and *mingshengqu* (scenic area). According to the Daikanwa Jiten, a standard reference on classical Chinese, *fengjing* (literally, winds and views) has been used to mean "scenery" since the Qin dynasty (221–206 B.C.E.), while `mingsheng—according to Wu (1992:68), a contraction of *ming shan sheng di* (famous mountains and unexcelled places)—has been used to refer to a place with beautiful scenery since the Northern Qi dynasty (550–577 C.E.). From the work of historian Timothy Brook and art historian James Cahill, we know that by the sixteenthth century, when leisure travel became a culturally approved activity for the gentry (Teng 2001; Brook 1998:180), a "national" canon of *mingsheng* had been well established by a succession of literati who, during their visits, referred back to the impressions of their predecessors, particularly Tang and Song (618–1279) scholar-officials and cultural heroes such as Li Bo, Du Fu, Ouyang Xiu, Lu You, or Su Shi (see Strassberg 1994). These earlier travel writings—whether prose or poetry—were reflections on official or family-occasioned journeys or short leisure outings, and they documented the inscriptions (a sort of scholarly graffiti) their authors and others had left at the sites (fig. 2). These inscriptions were also circulated in the form of rubbings and included in gazetteers.

Pei-yi Wu characterizes the "usual content" of sixteenth-century travel accounts (*youji*) as "making the rounds of the historical sites and scenic spots, all cataloged and celebrated in earlier writings" (Wu 1992:70). Locally, scenic spots had been assembled into sets of views (*jing*) with captions, some of which were circulated as woodblock prints, such as the "Twenty Views of Jinling" (Nanjing) in Gu Qiyuan's (1565–1628) *On Refined Travel* (*Ya you pian*; Teng 2001:64). Brook (1998:59) describes the *jing* (or "prospect," as he translates it) as "an established and well-defined view onto a known landscape, not a view that the artist selects and defines himself." Indeed, in a number of cases, artists produced sets of views relying on established schemata with-

FIG. 2. Inscribing a Cliff, 1609. Reproduced from Strassberg (1994, inside front cover).

out having visited the site (Cahill 1992:281). Graphic and textual representations of scenic spots constituted a single canon; poets writing about a particular spot would use the sets of views as subjects for a poem cycle (Brook 1998:59). As James Cahill (1992:252) writes, "Received information and recognition of named places seem to have somewhat supplanted firsthand observation of untouched nature" and resulted in paintings of rocks and cliffs that more closely resembled the objects they were named after (such as a lotus or a tiger) than their actual appearance (279). Literati traveled to confirm what they had already been expected to know from images and texts (280); they followed the same itinerary from one named place to another, noting inscriptions on steles and cliffs (Wu 1992:82–83) and the resemblance of peaks and rocks "to a tiger or a drunken man" (Cahill 1992:251). Their responses to sights were "more often didactic than introspective, and the companions and their pronouncements [were] duly noted" (Wu 1992:68). Views—even in their names—encompassed not only a particular aspect of a scenic spot, along with the poetic or historical references it should evoke, but also the appropriate circumstances of viewing, which could include season, time of the day, weather, and the spectator's mood.

So well was the canon established that when a particular traveler did not get to see certain spots, he would often record and enumerate those he had missed (Wu 1992:70). Sets of views and poems were produced both for promotional purposes, to surround a city with a cultural aura and set up an itinerary for visits, and as souvenirs sold at street stalls (Cahill 1992:255–56). Some of the most common views would be immediately identifiable as a particular location from the way in which they were composed: thus "[s]cholars in a boat beneath a cliff inevitably signified journeying to Red Cliff," as described by Su Shi, and "poets seated along a winding stream with floating winecups was instantly recognized as the gathering at the Orchid Pavilion" immortalized in a 353 C.E. anthology of poetry (Strassberg 1994:7).

The canon of scenic spots was reproduced in official county gazetteers and gazetteers created for the scenic areas—such as famous mountains or gardens—themselves (Brook 1998). Gazetteers were published into the 1930s, and the tradition was later renewed by local governments after 1978. These newly compiled gazetteers reproduced the canon and often added new scenic spots in keeping with traditional conventions of categorization, naming, and description. For example, the gazetteer for the famous sacred Mount Emei in Sichuan, published by the provincial government in 1996 and complete with an English table of contents, provides descriptions of the "Traditional Ten Views" from "Evening Bells at the Holy Temple" (Sheng si wan zhong) to the "Auspicious Halo at Golden Summit" (Jinding xiang guang), followed by a series of similarly named "New and Remote Views and Spots." It then provides short descriptions of individual mingsheng, classified into the following categories: mountains, famous and old trees, stones, caves, slopes, waters, bridges, pavilions, and inscribed steles (Sichuan Province

1996:171–222). Temples and monasteries are treated in a separate chapter entitled "Religion." The order of the categories largely parallels the previous gazetteer (Yinguang 1934, v. 1, *juan* 3), which in turn follows earlier ones.

Latter-day gazetteers are very much an antiquarian genre, with little direct impact on tourism—though indirectly they still affect, and certainly reflect, the tourist canon. But their tradition lives on in promotional literature for tourists and popular media representations of travel.

In the late nineteenth and early twentieth centuries, when guidebooks with a focus on practical information had become a staple for middle-class European travelers (Koshar 2000; Palmowski 2002), "guidebooks" of Beijing and even Shanghai, with all its Western influences, had more in common with fifteenth-century albums of views than with Baedeker or other European guidebooks of the time. Though the *Concise Notes on the Capital* (Dumen jilüe 1864), the *Shanghai Miscellanea* (Hu you zaji 1876), the *Illustrated Grand Sites of Shanghai* (Shenjiang shengjingtu 1884), and their numerous followers go beyond the traditional views of these cities to include new architecture and sites of commerce, Chinese literary historian Catherine Yeh has shown that they remain a pastiche of prints and poetic captions. In the *Shanghai Miscellanea*, entries for "roadside trees," "horse races," "Natural History Museum," "Bureau for Smallpox Inoculation," and "sprinkler truck" follow each other in "happy serendipity." Contrary to the positivist exactness that the contemporary Western reader had come to expect from guidebooks—even from English-language guides to Shanghai—in these volumes,

no building is connected to a street; and no street is introduced with its architecture. And, Shanghai is a city without past. . . . All packed into the present, this city is a live performance of itemized and decontextualized tidbits . . . a theme park . . . a center of voyeuristic amusement. (Yeh 2006)

These books, with no practical information and a "high register language" (Yeh 2006) reminiscent of gazetteers, were published so that—as the preface to the *Illustrated Grand Sites of Shanghai* puts it—"gentlemen of refined tastes" "who have not been to Shanghai could enjoy its scenery."[5] They adjusted to modernity not by abandoning the "cameo gaze" of gazetteers and literati travel but, as Yeh shows, by expanding it from views (*jing*) of "famous scenic sites and ancient relics [*mingsheng guji*]" to a broader range of curiosities (*qi*) that can include technology, human spectacle, and food. By the early twentieth century, Baedeker was urging the tourist to free herself from the standardization of sites by offering as much information as she needed to get by on her own (Koshar 2000:127). Chinese guidebooks were standardizing new kinds of sights.

After the establishment of the Republic of China, publications such as the *Encyclopedia of Scenic Sites and Ancient Relics in All China* (Zhonghua quanguo mingsheng guji daguan) represented an effort to catalog the *mingsheng* within the new nationalist project of creating a sense of common Chinese heritage and contained an addendum on the "Scenic Sites of the World." Nonetheless, the introduction once again justified the project by referring to the travels of Tang and Song scholar-officials to "famous mountains and great rivers" (Gu 1922).

Scenic Spots and Nation-Building in Late State Socialism

After the war, the Communist takeover, and the Cultural Revolution (1966–1976), reemerging travel literature reached back to the scenic-spot tradition once again. The state, which strove to relegitimate itself by embarking on a promotion of previously derided "Chinese culture," played an important role.[6] Long before domestic tourism started, the journal *Tourist*, launched in 1979 by the Beijing Tourism Press, and numerous other magazines that followed brought back into circulation "the 108 views" of Mount Qingcheng and the idea of travel as "Climbing Famous Mountains, Listening to Legends, Contemplating Beautiful Views" (Wang Chunwu 1982). While *Tourist* was a popular magazine, the more highbrow *Travel Literature* (Lüyou wenxue), launched in Kaifeng in 1983, reprinted classical travel literature and attempted to revive the genre in the present (Strassberg 1994:427 n.23). Whether it was a well-known place like Guilin or a less well-known one like Mount Erxi in Hunan, readers were reminded of the poems written about them, famous quotes and steles left behind by literati travelers, and rocks shaped like Avalokitesvara (Tang 1982; Zhang Dalin 1982; Xiang 1982). A 1988 publication lists twenty-eight tourism magazines and newspapers, including one entitled *Scenic Views and Spots* (Fengjing mingsheng) (Shandong 1988:109–19).

New albums of views were put together to demonstrate the revival of tradition, such as the beautifully designed bilingual *Pictures and Poems of Mount Emei's Ten Sceneries* (Emei shi jing tu shi), by seal engraver Tian Chengke (1981), an octogenarian who had studied under famous pre-war artists. Classical poems on *mingsheng* (e.g., Xiao and A Hua 1992) and prose travel writings (see Strassberg 1994:427 n.23) were published in anthologies. Names of famous views from classical accounts, such as "A Thread of Sky" (Yi xian tian), were recycled at other sites. Key sites were restored—in the case of many buildings, this meant constructing them anew—and, in a tradition previously absent in China and introduced from the Soviet Union, statues of cultural heroes associated with the sites were erected at some of them, such as that of Su Shi at the Red Cliff in Hubei or that of General Li Bin at the Dujiangyan Dam. Reenactments of historical ceremonies at famous sites spread (Sofield and Li 1998:378). Some structures of iconic cultural significance were "restored" even though they had disappeared long before and their site was no longer exactly known. This was the case of the Orchid Pavilion, the place of a celebrated poets' gathering in the fourth century, which was "recreated" at a location in Zhejiang inferred from the *Collected Poems from the Orchid Pavilion*, next to a winding stream as described in the preface to that book (Strassberg 1994:7). Traditional views of landscape and architecture spread by means of wall calendars and postage stamps, reaching tens of millions (Petersen 1995:149). In the nineties, for the first time, television began conveying the same images to the majority of the Chinese population, and today they are reproduced on countless Internet sites.

As a result, recognizing representations of *mingsheng* and identifying some cultural references associated with them once again became part of a shared cultural grammar. The desire to travel could once again be the desire to validate one's knowledge of canonical representations, and this was now true for a much larger part of Chinese society, one which was poorly versed in the literati tradition beyond its superficial signs and had no code of travel behavior at its disposal. The new consumer economy attempted to offer solutions for this problem: in a Shanghai bookshop in 2002, I saw a coffee-table photo album of Zhangjajie, a popular scenic spot in the mountains of Hebei, in which the text and the captions under the photos were provided but the photos themselves had to be inserted by the reader. In this new version of the classical album, the reader's job was only to use his camera in the right places.[7]

For the new readership, the language of travel had changed from classical Chinese to the contemporary vernacular, and the sets of cultural associations had to be simplified and updated. Other changes were made in accordance with the government's ideology of modernization, nationalism, and socialism. Some of the sites were named Patriotic Education Sites. Mount Tai, historically one of the most-traveled sacred mountains, was endowed with new nationalistic and revolutionary meanings as—in the words of a 1993 gazetteer—"a base area for people's resistance against oppression, tyranny, and invasion" by erecting obelisks and mausolea (quoted in Dott 2002). In 1991, Prime Minister Li Peng added his inscription at Mt. Tai to those by the famous Tang poets Du Fu and Li Bo (Dott 2002). At the tomb of the Song general Yue Fei—a National Patriotic Education Site rebuilt in 1979—kneeling statues were erected of three "traitors" who conspired against Yue Fei with invaders from the "non-Chinese" Jin empire. The statues were surrounded by a cage-like fence, reminiscent of a pillory and bearing a sign reading, "Do Not Spit at the Statues."

Among the travels of famous literati, a new emphasis was added to those that had to do with Taiwan or the special economic zone of Hainan, newly developed and in need of cultural patina (e.g., *Tourist* 1982; Li Feng 1982). Both places had been outside the traditional travel canon but were now, for different reasons, important for the government: Taiwan as the subject of a campaign to prove that it was part of China, and Hainan as one of the first special economic zones. In another contested peripheral region, Xinjiang— a province with a large Turkic population and a history of resistance against Chinese domination—a mountain was discovered that was claimed to be the exact resemblance of Mao Zedong lying in state in his mausoleum, and it was renamed after him (Anagnost 1997:175). This scenic spot, while ostensibly natural, was thus themed to remind its viewers of another *mingsheng*, Mao's mausoleum in the capital. In all three cases, the state invoked traditional interpretive techniques of literati travel to extend to ambiguous regions the boundaries of what could be claimed as historical Chinese landscape. Something similar happened to the friendly "socialist" country Cuba during then-Chairman Jiang Zemin's visit there in 2001. Jiang presented Fidel Castro with a quatrain based on Li Bo's classic poem, "Early Leave from the White Emperor's Citadel" (Zao fa Baidicheng), written during his trip through the Three Gorges of the Yangzi in 759.[8] The quatrain was repeatedly broadcast in the mass media.

In addition to celebrating the rehabilitation of the canon of literati travel, the reconstruction of some monasteries and palaces destroyed in the Cultural Revolution, and the refurbishing of some of them as sites of patriotic education, some newly declared *mingsheng* were added to the canon. These included revolutionary and nationalistic memorial sites as well as modern constructions such as bridges and high-rises.

This new catalog of *mingsheng* appeared in a number of publications in the late 1980s. The *Index of Scenic Areas of China* (Zhongguo mingsheng suoyin), very similar in its organization to the 1922 *Encyclopedia of Scenic Sites and Ancient Relics in All China* (Zhonghua quanguo mingsheng guji daguan), lists

old revolutionary sites; famous mountains and unexcelled waters; strange rocks and weird caves; Buddhist monasteries and Taoist observatories; pagodas, statues, and stone monuments; palaces, parks, and groves; pavilions, terraces, towers, and mansions; walls, castles, bridges, and forts; tombs, mausolea, steles, and arches. (Li Wenfang 1987, inside front cover)

Later varieties of such publications expanded the boundaries of *ming-sheng* further, including not only museums and zoos but also theme parks, all the while largely retaining the language and organization of the material as well as the state-approved canon (e.g., China Cultural Relics Association et al. 1998). The creation of a structure of cultural references for scenic sites—following the literati model but with an updated repertoire—was reflected upon in a proposal at the conference of the China Travel Literature Research Association in 1990, where it was asserted that "contemporary landscape poetry should describe natural landscapes together with the heroic spirit of the Party leading the people in transforming mountains and rivers and the new face of mountains and rivers after the transformation" (Yu Xuecai 1991:60). The new master narrative of Chinese *mingsheng* was to unite into a seamless whole traditional landscapes of literati travel (reconfigured as proof of a rich national culture), landscapes symbolic of the Communist victory and the "birth of New China," and landscapes expressing China's reform-era economic modernization and rising standing in the world. As the *Conspectus of China's Scenic Sites* (Zhongguo mingsheng gailan) put it in 1999:

China has vast lands and abundant goods; it is an ancient civilization of 5,000 years; over the long course of various historical eras, [its] industrious and wise people of all nationalities have created a glorious history and culture. These are embodied in the Fatherland's (*zuguo*) mountains and waters, architecture, water conservation projects, parks, and tombs. (Yong 1999, *shang juan*)

As Tim Oakes writes in his pioneering study of tourism and modernity in Guizhou, in southwestern China, the state took an active role in shaping and promoting the new canon as it attempted to "fix the boundaries of a unique and essential China, a nation equal and unique among a modern community of nations" (Oakes 1998:48). In 1982, it created a system of National and Provincial Key Scenic Areas (*zhongdian fengjing mingshengqu*). The 1988 *Encyclopedia of National Key Scenic Areas*, which follows the old structure of pictures and descriptions, states that these places are the "shared treasure and wealth of the Chinese race [*Zhonghua minzu*]" and serve as sites of "patriotic education" (Ministry of Urban Construction and Environmental Protection 1988).

But the development that probably did the most to strengthen the new canon of a national landscape was one in which the market played as large a role as the state. This was the "theme park fever," which Oakes identifies as "the beginning of tourism's active collaboration in the project of Chinese modernity, only the most obvious aspect of which is the . . . commercialism and commodification that have combined to invent a nostalgic past upon which to build a sense of national identity and alternative modernity" (Oakes 1998:50).

In the 1990s, an estimated 2,000 to 2,500 amusement and theme parks, most of them based on "folk customs" and themes from Chinese history, sprang up in China's cities. There were 260 theme parks based on the popular vernacular novel, *Journey to the West* (Xi you ji), alone (Ap 2003:195–97). Visiting them became a proto-tourist activity for many people: it familiarized them with representations of traditional *mingsheng* historically known only to a small literati elite and taught them to see these as parts of a national landscape. The parks also prepared visitors for the experience of traveling to these sites and taught them how to consume the sites when they encountered them.

The first and most written-about major theme park, Splendid China in Shenzhen, opened in 1989 and includes in its display twelve miniaturized landscapes from the traditional canon plus forty-eight famous man-made structures, from the Great Wall to the Potala in Tibet. The park also contains ensembles of altogether 65,000 pottery figurines, ranging from a "memorial ceremony for Confucius" to "ethnic village scenes" such as Mongol archers on horseback. The figures are, as a promotional brochure from the park puts it, "harmoniously and skillfully integrated with the scenic attractions to form a pleasing whole, expressing the cream of glorious culture and long history of the Chinese nation" (quoted in Stanley 1998:66–67). In another Shenzhen theme park, China Folk Culture Villages, opened in 1991, ethnicity became the main theme, reinforced by regular performances by members of "minorities" who live in their respective "villages" in the park—

much like Indians and Bedouins at the 1893 Chicago World's Columbian Exposition—and wear their "ethnic costume." Visitors too can rent "ethnic clothing" and participate in the "ethnic dances" (Stanley 1998:68).

Parts of China's landscape were thus reinterpreted as both national and ethnic, a configuration in which—as Oakes noted when writing about theme parks in Southeast Asia—culture and ethnicity are tied to current administrative divisions, inventing "regional cultures as selective traditions of essential (and unique) folk quaintness." In this process, "parts which contribute to the construction of an imagined multicultural community get salvaged and preserved" (Oakes 1998:36–37), whereas "those deemed too primitive or emphasizing local ethnic identity should be eradicated" (Picard 1993:93, quoted in Oakes). The spread of representations of "ethnic minorities" as exotic and fascinating "internal Others" formed an important theme in reform-era media and literature (Gladney 1994; Schein 1997) and resulted in a kind of "salvage orientalism," reflected in a Party injunction to promote ethnic cultural festivals and encourage attendance at them (Sofield and Li 1998:373; Mueggler 2002). The foregrounding of the ethnic exotic and the fusing of landscape with "minority" folklore was an element of the new canon that spurred a growth industry in tourism development in the 1990s, making spectacles of "minority customs" an almost *de rigueur* element in any tourist itinerary, aside from some metropolitan ones (Sofield and Li 1998:371– 76; Oakes 1998:135–87; Tan et al. 2001:93–215; Hyde 2001). Certain ethnicities, just like scenic spots, acquired a standard set of cultural references: any representation of the Miao would include a tune on the *lusheng* pipe; Mongolians would always ride horses and wrestle; and Tibetans would always be associated with *hada* shawls, prayer flags, and the "eternal plateau" (Xu Xinjian 2001:209).

In addition to reproducing *en masse* a canon of sites and attaching new cultural references, such as ethnicity, to some of them, the theme parks also situated the national landscape in a global perspective. They did so not only by juxtaposing parks based on themes from Chinese history with others representing famous landscapes and buildings from other parts of the world— like Window on the World in Shenzhen—but also by furnishing Chinese sites with cachets of approval from an imagined global hierarchy: "the world's biggest palace," "the world's largest Buddha," "the world's most splendid building located at the highest land above sea level," "the world's longest rampart," and the "world's oldest Ancient Star Observatory," for example (Sofield and Li 1998:381–82). Such epithets serve to indicate that *mingsheng* now represent not only a shared heritage of a heroic past but also proof of China's superiority over other nations by virtue of that past.

But theme parks do not only represent *mingsheng*: they have, as mentioned earlier, become *mingsheng* themselves. The 1999 *Conspectus of Chinese Scenic Sites and Ancient Relics* has entries on three theme parks in Shenzhen alone, describing, for example, China Folk Culture Villages as reflecting "the glorious and resplendent history and culture of the Chinese race and its unfading attractiveness" (*Zhonghua minzu guanghui canlan di lishi ji qi bu xiu di meili*) (Yong 1999, xia juan:1391). In the Chinese tourist imagination, the differentiation between the ("inauthentic") reproduction and the ("authentic") site—an important distinction in Western tourist discourse (MacCannell 1976:44)—is much less clear. Sofield and Li (1998:384) suggest that for visitors to the China Folk Culture Villages, the "inhabitants" of the villages engage in, rather than just act out, their "traditional" lifestyles. Oakes quotes a tourist as saying that "because Shenzhen has its Splendid China, it also has history." He also describes the naming of a star discovered by a Chinese observatory after Splendid China, with the justification that "Splendid China collects all the best of the Chinese people" (Oakes 1998:51).

In sum, the late socialist Chinese state reinscribed the national territory with a cultural canon that claimed historical continuity yet was modified in particular ways, notably by the ethnicization of the national geography and the nationalization of modernity, which had in earlier times appeared only in the culturally ambiguous geography of Shanghai. In doing so—and embracing the budding media of popular culture for the purpose—the Chinese state prepared its citizens for being tourists in a number of fairly idiosyncratic ways that were absent in other late socialist states. I will return to this observation and explore the reasons underlying it in chapter 3.

Scenic Spots in the Era of Commercialized Tourism

When large-scale domestic tourism emerged, traditional *mingsheng* remained at the core of tourist routes. To reinforce that, entire counties have been renamed after the famous mountains Emei in Sichuan and Wuyi in Fujian, as well as after the Stone Forest in Yunnan. In the early 2000s, an American student applying for a job as bartender on one of the Yangzi cruise ships was asked during his job interview to recite a poem by Li Bo, one of the poets most strongly connected to the historical canon of Yangzi sites.[9] But in the economic boom of the 1990s and 2000s, new sites were eager to compete.

Although they represented a much more diverse array of places, the recipe for their "enshrinement" (MacCannell 1976:44–45) was standard and in line with the conceptual framework of the *mingsheng*. Their developers worked hard to bound and catalog the sites and to conjure up cultural references and invent cultural practices supposedly specific to each site.

Expanding the Canon

The essays in *Tourism, Anthropology and China* (Tan et al. 2001) describe how tourist attractions have come to include the birthplaces of Confucius and Mao, houses of Communist writers and Hong Kong actresses, hill crests named for their supposed resemblance to Disney figures, and "ethnic" villages supposedly practicing "matriarchy;" folk ballad performances and re-enactments of fishing with cormorants; and the "Hawaii of China" (Hainan) and "Mini-Europe in the Orient" (Qingdao, with its German architecture).

Hardening Boundaries

While the conceptual boundaries of *mingsheng* expanded, their geographical boundaries were made more visible. Even "old towns" (*gu zhen*)—such as the "water towns" (*shuixiang*) around Shanghai or "reconstructed" areas in big cities, such as the Yu Garden in Shanghai—or lakeshores, such as the Kuku Nor in Qinghai, were equipped with ticket gates and fences (fig. 3).

Cataloging and Naming Views

Where no set canon of views had existed, views were identified and enumerated. In the Fuxing (Revival) Park in Shanghai, originally set up in 1909 by the French, the "main scenic spots" listed on large signs at the entrance include both the 1985 statues of Marx and Engels and the "French-style sunken flowerbed." Natural formations were named—borrowing names from other sites or using ethnic or mythical references—and the names became brands promoted in newly composed "folk songs" as well as on cigarette labels.

Adding Cultural References

"Ancient-looking" but highly standardized buildings were erected in the "old towns" and in "ethnic villages," following crude models of the "Ming-Qing

FIG. 3. *The gate of the "old town" of Zhujiajiao, Jiangsu. Photo by author.*

house," the "Tibetan-style house," or the "Qiang watchtower," according to the ethnic theming of the area (but not necessarily corresponding to the village's actual ethnic makeup). Inhabitants of some "ethnic villages," such as those on Lugu Lake in Yunnan, were required to wear "ethnic clothing," even if they were ethnically Han (Walsh 2001).

Performing the Spot

Song and dance performances, presented as ethnic, historical, religious or simply rural folklore, and re-enactments of religious ceremonies and traditional "ethnic" festivals and "customs," ranging from courtship rituals to archery contests, emerged as a new standard fixture of tourism. These performances succeeded view albums and poems as cultural master narratives of the scenic spots presented in an easy-to-digest form. Some performances are indoors, while others take place amidst street festivities and crowds of young hostesses dressed in uniforms that usually combine elements of "traditional" dress—"ethnic" costume or the *cheongsam*, the tight slit robe developed in Shanghai in the early twentieth century—with the ribbons of American cheerleaders and the tights and shoes of teenage Soviet gymnasts. Beneath the veneer of a generic Orientalist instrumentation, the music and choreography appear to reach back to 1950s Soviet orchestral arrangements of "folk" music and patriotic songs, which, with their conservative musical phraseology and their alternation between maternal-feminine sweetness and muscular-masculine pathos, served as the model for the formation of a national Chinese performing art in the early Communist period.[10] (In the Soviet Union, "ethnographic evenings" were put to use as a way of "getting to know the peoples of the USSR" from as early on as the 1920s; see Hirsch 2003:695.)

Yet the most direct inspiration from which the song and dance performances in China draw is unquestionably disco, manifested not only in the simple, melodious, and rhythmical tunes, the dance movements reminiscent of Jane Fonda's aerobics, and the sound system, but also in the dark red hues and glittering crystal balls of the stage design. Sometimes references to disco are explicit, as in the "Oriental Disco" performance in the China Folk Culture Villages (Oakes 1998:55) or in the activity entitled "Disco dancing performed by bound-feet old ladies," performed as part of the "Mysterious Fuxian Lake" tour of "Yunnan ancient culture" and offered as a side activity of the 2002 Kunming International Tourism Festival (fig. 4).

Creating Festivals

Performances become particularly frenzied during the innumerable tourist festivals organized by local governments as a way to attract tourists. These range from the exhibition of ethnic "customs" (such as the Maidens Festival of the Tujia in Enshi, Hubei, or the horse races in Tongliao, inner Mongolia) to the "reenactment" of actual or supposed local traditions (such as the Qiantangjiang Tidal-Wave-Watching Festival in Hangzhou and the International Festival of Colored Sand Carving in Luliang, Yunnan). Religious rites, such as the International Cultural and Touristic Mazu Festival in Tianjin or the International Confucius Fest in Qufu, Shandong, and celebrations of historical myths (for example, the Zhaojun Cultural Festival in Hohhot, Inner Mongolia, held in honor of a Han dynasty (202 B.C.E.–220 C.E.) princess married off to a Hunnish ruler, or the sacrificial ceremony for Emperor Yan, the mythical ancestor of the Chinese, in Zhuzhou, Hunan) are mixed with

FIG. 4. *"Ethnic dancing" in front of the Stone Forest. Cover of* Guide to the Third Kunming International Tourism Festival, China *(Kunming: Organizing Committee of the Third Kunming International Tourism Festival, 2002). Author's collection.*

global fads, such as the International Dinosaur Lantern Festival in Zigong, Sichuan, and the International Beer Fest in Qingdao. But it is in the month-long annual Kunming International Tourism Festival in the capital of Yunnan, the province most strongly promoted through its ethnic minorities, that this packaging of ethnicity and culture-to-go reaches its head-spinning apotheosis. Here, as an English-language guide to the 2002 Festival attests, one can attend activities ranging from the "bride seizing activity of the Aini minority" to "worshipping Confucius," and from the "Water-splashing and Flower-picking Tourism Festival of Jinggu County" to the "appraisal and selection of the Ruili River Lady."

Most activities are participatory in the sense that performers and staff interact with viewers and encourage them to come on stage and perform some symbolic version of the activity, or just mingle and take photos with the performers. According to the Kunming festival brochure, visitors to the Mengbanaxi Ethnic Folk Customs Festival in Luxi are supposed to join "10 thousand people to pick flowers and meet friends," while at the Grand Nujiang Canyon, "recreation activities" are foreseen to include "piling sand on the loved ones." Tourists are encouraged to—and usually do—perform simplified religious ceremonies at temples or "ethnic" sites. In the "water towns" along the Grand Canal near Shanghai, tourists can buy fish at the waterside and release them in an act of Buddhist "merit-making."

Marketing Scenic Spots

Some examples drawn from promotional materials published by tourism authorities in 2002 and 2003 illustrate the features of the contemporary marketing of scenic spots. Promotional materials are structured in the gazetteer tradition of the pastiche, cataloging sites—from temples to theme parks—with photos and brief texts without setting up a geographic or historical relationship between them. We learn, for instance, that a site lies "in the midst of high mountains" or "on crystal clear waters,"[11] but most of the time we do not get any of the tectonic details that we've come to expect from Western travel literature, such as the height, name, or geological origin of mountains, or the names of rivers or lakes. Following a tradition started by early twentieth-century guidebooks, "local specialties" (tutechan) to taste and buy are included among the cameos. Thus, next to the section on the "Three Natural Wonders" at Mount Qingcheng in a brochure published by the Sichuan Province Tourism Administration, there appears a list of "Four Uniques," which turn out to be local dishes.

The brochures usually provide "suggested itineraries," and some contain lists of flights and trains to and hotels and restaurants in the capital of the province described. What most brochures do not contain is maps or travel information to the scenic spots themselves. The brochures are not intended to help travelers to get to a destination or plan a holiday. They are designed to whet the appetites of tourists, who will then have to turn to a travel agent to organize their visit.

The inside front cover of *Chengdu Travel Guide*, published by Sichuan Meishu Chubanshe in 1996 but distributed by the Chengdu City Tourism Administration, features the Chengdu World Landscape Park, with a photo of its developer with Yang Shangkun, a former Chairman of the People's Republic. The park is described as "the ultimate in cultural tourism sights in Western China" (26). The guide contains, in addition to traditional sites, numerous other theme parks and holiday villages. The description of Dujiangyan Dam, a World Cultural Heritage site constructed in the 3rd century B.C.E., includes Dujiangyan Huaxia Waxwork City, "the world's largest," which offers "wax images of commanding [*chicha fengyun*] emperors and kings from China's 5000-year history, a unique round swimming pool, a high-class sauna, a song and dance hall," etc. (67).

An English-language pamphlet entitled *Tour of Natural Scenary* [sic], published by the Guangdong Province Tourism Administration, has a more traditional focus on hundreds of scenic spots. The description of White Cloud Mountain Scenic Spot, a well-known historic *mingsheng* near Guangzhou, provides a contemporary set of views:

Many renowned poets and scholars of past dynasties have visited the place, and left poems and words. In recent years the scenic spot has set up new scenic spots and scenarios, such as White Cloud Ropeway, Ming Chun Gu, Yuan Tai Garden, White Cloud Slideway, which combining with the old sceneries, for example Looking Afar in Evening from White Cloud Mountain, The First Peak Under the Southern Sky, Wind Soughing [sic] in the Pines, . . . made White Cloud Mountain the most ideal place for sightseeing. (4)

For a lesser-known National Key Scenic Area, Xiling Mountain near Chengdu in Sichuan, a 2003 Chengdu city map published by the National Tourism Administration lists "three great curious sights [*qiguan*]": "Sunshine on Golden Mountain," "Borderline Between *Yin* and *Yang*," and "Buddha's Light in the Forest." These are described as "meteorological phenomena" but not explained further. "Curious sight" is an expression familiar from both pre-modern travel literature and early twentieth-century accounts of Western lifestyles in Shanghai (Yeh 2006).

The brochures present ethnic "minorities" as people who have never stopped singing and dancing. A pamphlet from Hunan says of the Tujia "nationality": "The contents of the dance reflect the work and life environment of local people and fully display the people's open, optimistic and passionate personality." Such infantilizing representations of minorities are common in Chinese media; tourists here are invited to experience a chapter from the great album of "nationalities" with the same sense of cultural recognition as they would a famous mountain.

Although official figures suggest that the share of organized tourism in China is, while growing, still lower than in the West—in 1998, it was reported to be 8 percent (Wei et al. 1999:149)—these figures are based on a comparison of travel agency statistics with the total number of domestic trips taken. It appears that the share of group tourism within domestic tourism to scenic spots outside large cities is very high. In fact, research in Lijiang and Lugu Lake in Yunnan suggests that group travel is higher among domestic than foreign tourists (Duang 2000; Walsh and Swain 2004). Tourist itineraries offered by travel agencies feature the same attractions as the promotional literature reviewed above, and they frame them in the same way. For example, an advertisement in the Shanghai newspaper *Travel Times* for a tour to Ningxia offered by Shanghai Heping Guoji Lüxingshe runs as follows:

Visit the mysterious pyramids of the Orient: the mausoleum of the Xixia kings. Tour the Royal Mausoleum Museum, the Wax Images Museum, the ruins of the imperial tombs. En route, you can visit the largest cinema city of the Northwest . . . and the Sand Lake, a national AAAA level scenic spot.

Travel by train to Shapotou Scenic Spot in the desert (sand surfing, camel riding, rafting on the Yellow River on sheepskin rafts at an added charge) . . . Visit Gaomiao, the national key cultural protection unit that unites Buddhism, Confucianism and Taoism. Bus to the Tonghu grasslands in Inner Mongolia (yurts). Enjoy the scenery, songs, wine, hada, eat mutton by hand, participate in a campfire banquet (songs and dances at extra charge). (Lüyou shibao, July 11, C4)

These glossy brochures and catalogs published by tourism authorities, travel agencies, and site developers have been much more important in shaping the tourist's imagination than guidebooks, which did not become popular until around 2000. In addition to brochures, television, and festivals, the canon of scenic spots circulates in announcements made on airplanes and trains before arriving in a city and in videos played in buses. By contrast, guidebooks are sold exclusively in bookshops, and one sees very few Chinese tourists wandering around with a guidebook in hand.

The main direction of Chinese tourism development in the years of quasi-market economy has been the commercialization of the scenic spot canon. The following chapter shows the narrative and visual impulses that frame the consumption of two highly popular mainstream scenic spots in today's China: one that is part of the traditional canon, and another that has been recently developed. The tourist's experience of these two sites is contrasted with that of a town lying between them, a town which is not a scenic spot for Chinese tourists but is popular with Western backpackers. In these encounters, we see the complex ways in which the development of tourist sites, driven by commercial considerations, remains enmeshed with meanings and interpretations established simultaneously and earlier by state orthodoxy.

2

TWO SITES AND A NON-SITE

Mounts Emei, Jiuzhaigou, and Songpan

S ichuan Province is part of the historical heartland: it is associated with cultural and political heroes from Li Bo to Deng Xiaoping and has a wealth of historic *mingsheng*, including the sacred Mount Emei, the Three Gorges of the Yangzi, and Leshan, with its giant Buddha statue (fig. 5).

A Classic Revisited: Mount Emei, 2002

While new tourist sites have sprung up, historic *mingsheng* too have been bounded, ticket gates constructed, and the tourist experience "modernized." In 2002, when I visited Mount Emei—one of the four traditional sacred mountains in Chinese Buddhism, immortalized by a long line of literati, including Li Bo, whose poem was printed on the ticket—I had to make my way through a huge "transportation center" at its foot. While groups of cane-carrying elderly women pilgrims in cotton shoes still climbed the mountain, most tourists, having purchased a ticket, were taken to the cable car in air-conditioned buses, in which a DVD player provided an introduction to the "Ten Views of Emei." Then, apparently to enhance travelers' sense of the exotic, it played a few clips of "Tibetan songs" with images of the Potala, the Dalai Lama's former residence in Lhasa, even though there were no Tibetans in the area and the Buddhist tradition that canonized Emei was quite different from that of the Tibetans. Some passengers picked up the refrain

FIG. 5. *Deng Xiaoping visiting his native province: Inside front cover of* Travel Sichuan China *(Sichuan Tourism Administration). Author's collection.*

of one of the songs, "fair maiden," in Chinese (*meili di guniang*). The show finished with a mix of images—mountain landscapes, Buddha statues, Tibetans in folk costumes, and white tourists burning incense at temples— accompanied by the tune "Amazing Grace."

Halfway up the mountain, tourists had to buy (in addition to the admission ticket) a "walking ticket," which gave them the right to walk around. This ticket had the tourist's snapshot on it. On the path from the cable car to the summit, vendors hawked pairs of small locks locked into each other.

FIG. 6. "Love locks," a tourist attraction at Mount Emei. Photo by author.

They said this was a "two-thousand-year-old" tradition to ensure good luck for couples, but the couples that bought locks affixed them to the railing of a clearly recent statue in the shape of a pair of giant locks (fig. 6). While stone steles at every temple and pavilion explained their historic and literary significance, Tibetan-style songs blared from loudspeakers at a recently rebuilt temple on the summit.

The "Golden Route": A Trip to Jiuzhaigou

About 500 kilometers north of Mount Emei lies Jiuzhaigou, a 72,000–hectare nature reserve (*ziran baohuqu*) that comprises a cascade of pools and waterfalls carved into the karst of the Min Mountains in northern Sichuan, on the southern end of the Tibet-Qinghai plateau. Designated a national-level nature reserve in 1978, a National Key Scenic Area in 1982, entered in UNESCO's World Natural Heritage in 1992, and recognized as a National AAAA Scenic Area, Jiuzhaigou has been one of the "hottest" destinations for Chinese tourists in recent years. In 1999, the preface to the monumental *Conspectus of China's Scenic Sites* stated squarely that "the miraculous light emanating from Jiuzhaigou's lakes can indeed be called the number one water under heaven" (Yong 1999, *shang juan*). A video clip of Jiuzhaigou, accompanied by "Amazing Grace," is shown on many flights to Chengdu, the capital of Sichuan.

In addition to its scenic beauty, thus duly recognized by national and international authorities, Jiuzhaigou also has that other important tourist attraction, ethnicity, which Sichuan province began promoting as a tourism resource in the late nineties (Xu Xinjian 2001:203). Jiuzhaigou lies in the Aba (Ngawa) Tibetan and Qiang Autonomous Prefecture, which—as bilingual billboards on the way to Jiuzhaigou tell travelers—is striving to become "the most developed Tibetan region in China." The name Jiuzhaigou—"Nine Stockades Gap"—is derived from the nine villages on its territory, with an official population of about one thousand (Lindberg et al. 2003:121). In the English text of the Sichuan Tourism Administration's bilingual *Travel Sichuan China*, Jiuzhaigou is described as "famed the world over as the Dreamland and the Fairyland" that "boasts emerald green lakes, split-level waterfalls, rainbow-hued woods, snow-capped peaks and Tibetan folklores," collectively "referred to as the 'Five Souls of Jiuzhaigou'" (16). (We do not find out from the brochure, however, how high or in which mountains the place lies.)

Of all "minorities," Tibetans have a particular appeal for Chinese tourists, due to the Western image of Tibet as the Shangri-La of otherworldly landscapes and religious mystique, an image that has received wide currency in China since the late 1990s, even as it mixes with the usual dancing, singing, and drinking image of the "happily backward" minorities.[1] (A third set of imagery, in which Tibetans are not only backward but also aggressive, is more local, without national currency.)

What Jiuzhaigou does not have is history. Though also in Sichuan, it lies beyond the pale of the historical Chinese landscape, on the periphery of historical China itself. There are no cultural references to Jiuzhaigou from before the latest period of Chinese history, the so-called reform era. In fact, "Jiuzhaigou" as a geographical concept did not exist before 1978: it is absent from the 1924 Songpan County gazetteer's chapters describing routes, "mountains and rivers," as well as the administration of "barbarians." In terms of landscape and flora, Jiuzhaigou's scenery is more reminiscent of Yellowstone than of Mount Emei.

The Making of Jiuzhaigou

To establish Jiuzhaigou as a proper tourist site within the literati travel tradition, therefore, the Sichuan Province Tourism Administration's brochure manufactures cultural references. It endows Jiuzhaigou with epithets (*cheng*) designed to project the historic aura and classical style of literati culture and place Jiuzhaigou next to historic *mingsheng*: "It has been said that 'having been to Huangshan, one no longer looks at mountains; having been to Jiuzhaigou, one no longer looks at waters' and [it has been] called 'the king of China's water views'" (*you "Huangshan guilai bu kan shan, Jiuzhai guilai bu kan shui" he "Zhonghua shui jing zhi wang" zhi cheng*, 16).

As a national-level nature reserve, Jiuzhaigou is under the administrative authority of the State Environmental Protection Administration in Beijing. (There are also provincial-, prefectural-, and county-level nature reserves.) But as a National Key Scenic Area, Jiuzhaigou simultaneously falls under the jurisdiction of cultural relic protection authorities. In fact, however, the management of the reserve, which controls its infrastructure development, reports to the prefectural government in Barkam (bypassing the administration of Jiuzhaigou—formerly Nanping—County, so renamed in 1998).

Both Chinese law and the conventions of UNESCO, of whose international biosphere reserve network Jiuzhaigou is part, prohibit tourism in the so-called core and buffer zones of nature reserves. An estimated 80 percent of China's nature reserves have, however, developed tourism in the 1990s (Lindberg et al. 2003:107). This is clearly related to the fact that the reserves receive very little funding from their supervisory agencies, which makes them more dependent on tourism even than those in other poor non-Western countries. Creating "world-class" scenic spots is more in line with officials' concern with development than is spending money on nature conservation, whose results are intangible in the short term: a 1997 survey found that 46 percent of the reserves never monitored the environment. In 1999, national-level nature reserves received US $113 per square kilometer, one-third less than the average for "developing countries." On the other hand, around half of the reserves' tourism revenues were divided between the local and central governments as tax (Lindberg et al. 2003:108–16).[2]

Jiuzhaigou was "opened" for tourism in 1984, but at that time the return trip from Chengdu took seven days. In 1996, a new road was opened, which shortened the trip to two days one way. The tourist boom began in 1999, after a strong marketing campaign by the management and the prefectural government. Despite the difficulty of getting to Jiuzhaigou, by 1999 it was, with almost six hundred thousand visitors (up from 180,000 in 1997), the second most-visited nature reserve in the country.[3] It was also the only one that financed its entire budget from tourism revenue (Lindberg et al. 2003:108). Ticket sales alone brought in ¥47 million in 1999, equivalent to one-quarter of the year's total national budget for nature reserves. Of that, the reserve paid taxes of ¥12 million to the county government, accounting for 80 percent of its annual revenue.[4] In 2002, a Shanghai trade newspaper, *Travel Times* (Lüyou shibao), called the Jiuzhaigou tour "the golden route" of Chinese tourism (*Travel Times* 2002:D1).

Though—as confirmed by a manager at one of Sichuan's largest travel agencies in 2003[5]—Jiuzhaigou has become Sichuan's top tourist destination, "Greater Jiuzhai," which encompasses the nearby World Natural Heritage reserve Huanglong, remains on both the National and the Sichuan Tourism Authorities' lists of priority tourism development projects,[6] and an airport— built with money from the government and private investors—began serving the two sites only just in time for the "golden week" that followed the 1 October 2003 state holiday. (According to a local tour guide, the previous "golden week" had brought forty thousand visitors to the reserve each day.) The Ngawa Prefecture Tourism Administration's new bilingual brochure, published for the occasion, promotes "Greater Jiuzhai" as a region in which a tourist should do more than just visit Jiuzhaigou: "Fling into the arms of the prairie, taste the tenderness of the yellow Ri[v]er; Tracing the footmark of the Red Army, Releasing the passion of the youth" (English in the original). The brochure presents Jiuzhaigou and Huanglong on equal footing with two Long March memorial sites, a deer farm and "The Jiuzhai Paradise" ("Conference, vacation, honey moon and gymnasium").

What Is Not a "Voyage": The Journey

My colleague Joana Breidenbach and I visited Jiuzhaigou in September 2003, just before the opening of the airport. Getting to Jiuzhaigou by ground transportation on our own was not easy. All travel agencies in Chengdu offered three- and four-day package tours to Jiuzhaigou alone and to Jiuzhaigou plus Huanglong, respectively. This meant one day at each site, an arrangement typical of scenic spot tour packages (cf. Duang 2000; Walsh and Swain 2004). A package to Jiuzhaigou from China Travel Service, including transfer by bus, two nights at three-star hotels, and meals, cost ¥800 (around $90), a price affordable to a white-collar private sector or state employee from the coastal region. But a query about transportation without accommodation met with blank stares. Travel agency and hotel staff had not heard of any towns on the way to Jiuzhaigou, let alone public bus service to them. Staff at the Chengdu bus stations was unsure about buses in general and, when asked about Jiuzhaigou, advised us to get a package tour. The provincial tourism administration—a purely administrative body without an information service—did the same. Without a copy of the *Rough Guide* or *Lonely Planet China* or a visit to a backpacker Web site—offering "insider information" on local buses, trains, and hitchhiking—we had only two choices: purchase a package or charter a car with a driver. We did the former. (To go to Huanglong a year earlier, in August 2002, I had chartered a car.) Separately, I took an additional ride by public bus to Songpan, the last town on the way to Jiuzhaigou.

On the first day of our trip to Jiuzhaigou, our tour bus traveled ten hours from Chengdu to Chuanzhusi, a village in Songpan County where the roads to Jiuzhaigou and Huanglong fork. Our blue badges identified us as part of a China Travel Service group of twenty-one, all Chinese except the two of us. One man came from Taiwan, a group of three from Hong Kong. The others were young and middle-aged mainland Chinese. A group of coworkers from Hubei were coming from a conference; they were discussing transportation in Western China with the air of seasoned travelers. A Han man from Kashgar, Xinjiang, had also attended a conference in Chengdu, followed by a side trip to Tibet. He too was an experienced traveler: he had been to Vietnam for a sightseeing and beach holiday, as well as to Yunnan, always with groups, and had been once to Europe on a trip arranged by his employer. There were two younger couples: an English graduate from Guangzhou and his girlfriend; and a young woman with tight-fitting pastel-colored clothes and a shiny, heart-shaped wristwatch, reading a magazine with the English title LOVE, with her boyfriend.

Our guide, Xiao Ma, a young man, adjusted the microphone to achieve an echo effect popular with karaoke singers and began a rapid, schoolteacher-like staccato narrative in a formal register that was to continue through much of the ride, with frequent repetitions. As we left Chengdu, he told us that the city had 114 views, over two hundred "local snacks" (*tese xiaochi*), and 6,400 teahouses; that it was called "Paris of the East"; that it had the second-largest number of cars in China; and he quoted Li Bo, Du Fu, and "old sayings" about the city. The passengers on one side of the bus drew the curtains to keep out

FIG. 7. The Min River valley, Ngawa Prefecture, Sichuan. Photo by author.

the sun and dozed off or snacked while we passed the town of Dujiangyan, whose status as a National Historic and Cultural City was announced on a huge stone stele bearing the English inscription, "Tourist City of China."

After Dujiangyan, we entered Ngawa Prefecture and the valley of the Min River. To us, the view of the rapid river flanked by increasingly tall mountains was breathtaking, and the charm of the landscape was enhanced by the villages with their wooden houses, temples, mosques, flowers, and yellow cobs of maize drying on the roadside (fig. 7). But Xiao Ma's narration was ambiguous. He intoned that "Han and Tibetans live together in peace" and that "our tour has two names: Natural Scenery Voyage [ziran fengjing you] and Ethnic Customs Voyage [minzu fengqing you]," and then told us about the dress, building styles, legends, and wedding customs of the Qiang ethnic group unique to this area. He said nothing specific about the villages, however, commenting instead that the area was very "backward," so that we had to "prepare [ourselves] for the fact that people's living conditions in the places we will be visiting are extremely bad," referring in particular to the road and the food. Then he shifted to talking about the "four holy mountains of Ngawa" and the regional specialties: various teas, herbs, and apples.

As we approached our lunch stop—a new roadside hotel—Xiao Ma took a break and put on a DVD with "Tibetan" video clips, already familiar from Mount Emei. As Ya Dong, promoted on the DVD as the "founder of Tibetan folk music," sang his songs in Chinese about sorrowful maidens, highland wind, and snowcapped mountains, the screen showed people in Tibetan dress raising their arms and waving white hada, the silk scarves that are the most common symbols of "traditional Tibetan culture" in Chinese popular media (Upton 2002:108).

After lunch, we drove through Songpan, which, Xiao Ma told us, had been a market town on the Silk Road. It still has a large Muslim population, many old wooden houses, and a covered bridge inside the city gate—an area declared, in 1990, a Historic and Cultural Town of Provincial Fame. Yet Xiao Ma was brief on this: he was preoccupied with warning us against patronizing the vendors and restaurants in Chuanzhusi, our overnight stop. The reason, he explained, was that local vendors were "unreasonable" and "wouldn't let go" if a customer did not want to buy. Though we suspected that Xiao Ma was more concerned about the commission he would receive from scheduled shopping stops later on, he attempted to raise our vigilance against locals by going back to the point that "this is an extremely poor county" whose "minority" inhabitants "dislike hygiene. They only wash once, when they get married." These assertions appeared to contradict his earlier happy and colorful portrayal of minorities, but they applied only to the people of the untamed, undeveloped area we were passing. "Tomorrow evening," he consoled us, "we will learn about the traditions and customs of the Qiang and the Tibetans" in the ordered safety of the scenic spot, about their "food and drink culture, religious beliefs, dress, and dances. The Tibetans say that 'if they talk they sing, and if they walk they dance.'" Between Songpan and Chuanzhusi, Xiao Ma pointed out the Long March Memorial. We did not stop there, but many other tour buses do: the memorial—it too being a gated scenic spot—sold over 220,000 admission tickets in 2002. Before dinner, Xiao Ma implored us once more: "It's best if you don't go outside the hotel; just take a rest. Don't go to any of the shops. The women [vendors] are ethnic and savage [yeman]. If you say you don't like something they might make trouble for you."

Chuanzhusi, a small village where the development of hotels catering to Jiuzhaigou tourists began in 1997, now consists of a row of hastily built hotels

FIG. 8. *Entrance to the Jiuzhaigou scenic area, Sichuan. Photo by author.*

and restaurants, flanked by red and green plastic palm trees that glow at night. In the evening, the karaoke bar opposite our hotel, as well as the hotel itself, seemed full of prostitutes. The old houses had apparently been demolished. As the site of the new Jiuzhaigou-Huanglong airport, Chuanzhusi is poised to see even more development.

The next morning, our bus delivered us to the visitors' center at the entrance to the Jiuzhaigou reserve. We were to be back at the bus in about five hours' time.

The Natural Scenery Voyage: The Site

The entrance looked like a tollgate or a border crossing on a motorway and closely resembled the transportation center at Mount Emei (fig. 8). From the brass plaques, we learned that, in addition to the distinctions we had been aware of, Jiuzhaigou was on the "China *Mingsheng* Top 40" list and was a provincial-level "civilized work unit," a rating referring to hygiene and courtesy. Here we were to buy our tickets, one for the entrance and one for the "green bus." The entry of local buses and taxis into the reserve had been banned in 2000 in response to a UNESCO report recommending the establishment of an environmentally friendly "park-and-ride" system.[7] The "green buses," which ran through the reserve at regular intervals, were supposed to be powered with natural gas,[8] but the smell and color of their emissions suggested that "green" referred only to the color the buses had been painted. The admission ticket admonished tourists to observe detailed environmental protection rules and to "insist on the 'Five Particulars' and 'Four Beauties,'" the nature of which we were unable to glean from the guides on the "green buses." In any case, the environmental rules, which included a ban on smoking, seemed draconian by Chinese standards. In some places, there were separate rubbish containers for paper and glass.

The "green bus" climbed up the mountain on a road that, in the midst of being broadened and repaved, resembled a construction site. The guide, a young woman in Tibetan costume, told us about the scenic spots we passed: waterfalls, lakes, terraces. She explained their names, referring often to their similarity to some animal or mythical figure and linking them thus to a legend or to classical poetry; in one place, she pointed to the similarity of the view to a scene from A Journey to the West. The Upper Seasons Lake, she said, could be contemplated in all four seasons, whereas the Reclining Dragon Lake should be seen at sunrise, at sunset, and in moonlight. We had heard most of this from Xiao Ma during the morning ride to the park.

Most tourists rode to the end and then visited the scenic spots one by one as they descended back to the entrance. The route covered only a small part of the reserve. Our group did not visit the Tibetan villages inside Jiuzhaigou, which a few years earlier had been used to accommodate visitors and to put on song and dance shows (Xu Xinjian 2001:207). The spots, grouped into five scenic zones, were connected by a plankway that was elevated above the ground, but most spots also had a bus stop nearby. At the spots, the walkway broadened into viewing terraces, where tourists took photos (fig. 9). The names of the spots, such as Treasured Mirror Cliff, Panda Lake, and Reclining Dragon Lake, had been given by the reserve administration and were displayed and explained on large boards: in the geography of the reserve, they had overwritten the names of the Tibetan villages on its territory. Many signs also offered cultural interpretations of the natural features, such as: "Lotus Basin Waterfall . . . is like the lotus basin in a Buddhists temple. It is a symbol of

FIG. 9. *Photo-taking at a vista point in Jiuzhaigou. Photo by author.*

luck." Although all signs were trilingual (Chinese, English, and Japanese), we did not see a single non-Chinese tourist during the entire day. "You foreign friends tend to get off at Songpan and not to come in groups to Jiuzhaigou," confirmed Xiao Ma.

In the reserve, there was a large, shopping mall-like building of marble, glass, and tile, which served as a souvenir emporium and dining hall. Only set lunches were available here, recreating the experience of a hotel restaurant en route. In addition, local women sold souvenirs around some of the bus stops.

Although entirely created by tourism, the service area around the entrance was in fact vastly larger than any of the Tibetan villages in the area. It numbered over 120 hotels, almost all built in the last six years; some new ones were being constructed while others stood abandoned and partially pulled down. The construction boom had been facilitated by the closure of small hotels within the reserve itself in 2000, in part also responding to UNESCO concerns about the environment.[9] Visitors were no longer allowed to stay overnight in the reserve itself, although some Western backpackers still stayed at the homes of local Tibetans. We stayed at one of the newest and biggest

FIG. 10. *Grand Jiuzhaigou Hotel. Photo by author.*

hotels, the Grand Jiuzhaigou. Its staff—like all reserve staff that comes into contact with tourists—was from outside Jiuzhaigou and largely Han. Only the souvenir vendors, the rubbish collectors, the forest guards, and the cleaning women were villagers from inside the reserve.

The hotel's style, according to its promotional brochure, was "classic elegance with Tibetan palatial architecture." This meant that it was painted on its exterior with a geometrical pattern of off-white and dark red—a faint echo of the Potala Palace—and incorporated the same pattern into the design of the spacious lobby, whose marble, crystal, and gold finishing hid shoddy workmanship (fig. 10). Above the reception counter was the sine qua non of Chinese hotel modernity: four clocks showing the time in the national capital, Beijing (identical to the local time), as well as New York, London, and Tokyo. In the room, everything from the brass lighting/television/air conditioning control panel between the two beds to the combs in the bathroom displayed the same, unfailingly uniform modernity.

At our dinner table, the consensus was that the day had been too exhausting: someone suggested that tourists should be taken from spot to spot by bus. But two of our fellow travelers, who had been to Jiuzhaigou a number of years earlier, were happy about the changes. Talking about them, they readily slipped into the environmental discourse now often encountered in Chinese media and official statements (Litzinger 2004):

The first time we had to stay in the Tibetan village (inside the reserve) and walk everywhere on foot. The chopsticks were dirty; there was no meat; and it wasn't so ecological. . . . Since the park has its own buses and tourists are no longer allowed to stay inside, there is again fish in the lakes. Now there is sustainable development.

The Ethnic Customs Voyage: The Performance

Our second "voyage" was to take place after dinner. We were taken to the Ethnic Culture Night, presented by the Jiuzhaigou Nationalities Art Troupe in a concrete arena made up like a giant yurt. At the entrance, a hostess in Tibetan dress placed a *hada* on visitors' shoulders: we were reminded that it "has been blessed by the gods and is the Tibetans' way of showing welcome to visitors."

As is customary in China, the show was led in dialogue by female and male hosts who presented the introduction and the text between the performances. It covered the standard repertoire of an "ethnic culture" evening, providing a cultural master narrative of the place. This "culture," according to the narration at the show, consists of "solemn and mysterious religious rites, cheerful folk songs, and wild folk dancing," including alluded-to mating or drinking rituals. Although some songs were in Chinese, each song and dance was identified as either Tibetan or Qiang. The representation confirmed Gladney's observation that while minority women in China are invariably presented as highly feminine and sexualized, "when minority men are portrayed . . . they are generally exoticized as strong and virile, practicing strange and humorous customs, or possessing extraordinary physical abilities in sport, work, or the capacity to consume large amounts of alcohol" (Gladney 2002). To complete the picture, the Qiang and Tibetans were established as patriotic Chinese citizens through the song "China, I Love You" performed by a Tibetan singer.

Though some songs, with their more shrill harmonies and a cappella chanting, sounded closer to the "Tibetan music" marketed under world music labels in the West, the thrust of the musical representation was strikingly different: it covered the Oriento-Pop range from the Soviet-inspired through imitations of Hong Kong styles to disco. These were complemented by a

FIG. 11 (top). *Presenting a hada to a performer. Photo by author*
FIG. 12. *The audience dances with the performers at the Ethnic Culture Night in Jiuzhaigou. Photo by author.*

number of acrobatic dances. There was nothing obviously "ethnic" in most of the instrumentation or singing. It was the colorful costumes and the texts that made the "ethnic" nature of the performances clear. The jacket of the Jiuzhaigou Nationalities Art Troupe's souvenir video CD, which every visitor could take home, explained that the troupe "successfully develop[s] and exhibit[s] the Tibetan and Qiang folk culture with natural and pure village flavor."

In a ritualized appropriation of a perceived Tibetan tradition, members of the audience expressed their appreciation for solo singers by walking onto the stage and draping the hada they had received around the singer's neck (fig. 11). The Tibetan woman who had sung "China, I Love You" was among those who received the most hadas. At one point, the audience was invited and proceeded to participate in a drinking ceremony and then to dance with the dancers on the stage (fig. 12). The evening culminated in several bouts of an "ethnic" version of tug-of-war, in which the contestants were volunteers from the audience. The winner was changed into Qiang costume and participated in a mock wedding ceremony with a Qiang "maiden" from the troupe.

Early next morning, our bus set out for the return journey. Our companions were going on to Huanglong, but we would get off the bus in Chuanzhusi. The half-day to Chuanzhusi was punctuated by numerous shopping stops. Our companions—perhaps influenced by a long story by Xiao Ma about yaks as the embodiment of highland environmental purity—bought lots of food (including yak meat), a dagger, a cane, and crafts made of yak horn.

On the bus, the merry atmosphere of the previous evening continued. Xiao Ma introduced a Tibetan woman as a Jiuzhaigou worker taking a ride with us to Chuanzhusi; he asked her to sing as payment and then induced passengers to sing. One improvised a mating song addressing the hitchhiker: "Tibetan maiden, you are so fair. . . ." After performing two songs himself, Xiao Ma turned on a video, this time a somewhat gothic-disco take on Tibetan themes, with the obligatory backdrop of blue sky, snowcapped peaks, and green pastures with yaks. We saw the same scenes as we looked out the window, and the Tibetan hitchhiker led the passengers in a performance of a song just heard on the video.

From Chuanzhusi, we took a taxi to Songpan. The driver offered us a horse ride: as we were to find out, he had an idea of what foreigners want.

What Is Not a Site: Songpan

Although *Lonely Planet* praises Jiuzhaigou for its "spectacular scenery," "dazzling features," and "superb hikes," it is at least as enthusiastic about Songpan. "This bustling, friendly town merits a visit of its own," exclaims the 1996 edition; "[a] fair number of its old wooden buildings are still intact, as are the ancient gates. . . . Farmers and Tibetan cattle herders clop down the cobblestone streets on horseback" (849). The book is especially impressed with the horseback treks offered to surrounding "valleys and forests so pristine and peaceful that you may not believe you're still in China" (849). The 2000 edition of the upmarket German guidebook *Dumont Kunstreiseführer* also suggests "a longer stay" in Songpan for its "colorful market and picturesque streets with old wooden houses" and devotes to it about as much text as it does to Jiuzhaigou (335). Primarily for the horse rides, Songpan is a popular destination for Western backpackers.

Unlike Jiuzhaigou, Songpan is firmly on China's historical map. Prefaces to the county's 1924 gazetteer state that Songpan first appeared on maps in III B.C.E. It became an important military outpost from the Tang on, controlling the Qiang and Tibetan population of today's Ngawa Prefecture (then Songpan County), as well as access to Sichuan from the north (Songpan [1924] 1967:5, 31). The gazetteer not only contains numerous renderings of Songpan's Eight Views (228–40), but it also quotes lines from the Tang poets Du Fu and Li Shangyin that, it claims, refer to one of these, Xuebao Peak (123–25). Songpan's unusually well preserved North Gate (fig. 13) and the remaining parts of the wall were built in 1380, when a Ming general pulled in to "pacify" the Qiang (83). Songpan still has a spectacular mix of "ethnicity," which should work as an asset in tourism development. Elsewhere in Ngawa, a village renamed and promoted as the "First Village of Western Qiang" has been designated an Ethnic Arts Village by the National Cultural Relics Bureau (Xu Xinjian 2001:204–5). Yet surprisingly, Songpan is missing from Xu Xinjian's (2001) review of tourism development in Ngawa. Here, no one has organized ethnic performances. Indeed, for Xiao Ma, Songpan's old town—its status as a Historic and Cultural Town of Provincial Fame notwithstanding—was not a scenic spot but a drag. A growing number of individual Chinese tourists do come to Songpan for horse riding during the October "golden week," but mainstream domestic tourism drives right through the town. The few groups that stay here overnight on their way to or from Jiuzhaigou lodge at new hotels built just

FIG. 13. *The North Gate of Songpan, Sichuan. Photo by author.*

outside the town, not at the simpler ones in the historic core. Of the seventeen guidebooks covering Sichuan that were available in Chengdu and Lanzhou at the time of our trip (all published after 2000), only two mentioned Songpan as a destination.

What Is Not Development: Backpackers, Homespun Globalization, and Economic Change in Songpan

The deputy head of the county tourism bureau admits that the popularity of Songpan with foreigners is not the result of policy, but of the activity of two trekking companies. Guo Shang,[10] the general manager of the older company Shunjiang Horse Treks, and now an influential businessman, says he started his business in 1987, when Israeli and Swiss students came from Beijing and wanted to go horseback riding. Today the two trekking companies employ almost one hundred guides with their horses. The officials at the tourism bureau admit to being surprised by the appearance of foreign tourists, but, they say, they've gradually gotten used to it. In Guo Shang's words, the bureau's attitude toward foreign tourism has been "Nothing. They don't support it but don't oppose it either."

Gradually, the town developed a dependency on foreign tourism. When the SARS epidemic wiped out tourism to China in 2002, Jiuzhaigou and Huanglong—relying on domestic tourists—were unaffected, but Songpan's merchants were hit hard. Tourism revenue in the county has increased tenfold between 1996 and 2002, when it exceeded ¥250 million (around $28 million), and has become the largest sector in the county's economy. The phenomenal growth has been mainly thanks to tourism to Jiuzhaigou and Huanglong, as well as Chuanzhusi's hotels, which served over 440,000 guests in 2002; its restaurants and shops are the prime earners of tourism revenue. Nonetheless, the revenue from Songpan Town—with over 180,000 hotel guests—is about the same as that from ticket sales in Huanglong, where—according to the county government's statistics—over 870,000 visitors spent ¥89 million in 2002. Around 70,000 hotel guests in the county were foreigners, who stay chiefly in Songpan Town. This suggests that the status of Songpan as an international tourist destination, while unstated and low-key, has nonetheless made a significant contribution to tourism's overall economic effect on the town, an effect that is comparable in terms of revenue to that at Huanglong, one of the most-visited nature reserves in China.

Tourism has left its mark on the town, but in a way that is very different from a scenic spot. The Internet café that advertises broadband connection and displays the English sign "English, Korean, Vietnamese, Aradic" [sic] comes as a surprise to travelers arriving in the small central area after the ten-hour trip from Chengdu. Agents from two companies approach foreign visitors, distributing business cards printed in English and offering horse treks. They are the locals so distrusted by Xiao Ma; but unlike him, they speak English, having learned it from their clients. The trekking companies' signs display English-language recommendations from *Lonely Planet* instead of titles granted by Chinese tourist authorities: indeed, their destinations, Erdao Hot Springs and Zhaga Waterfall, are nowhere to be found in Chinese travel brochures, not even the one published by the Songpan Tourism Bureau. Emma's Kitchen—"the best Pizza in Songpan"—is wallpapered with postcards sent by foreign backpackers (fig. 14) and offers an English-language book swap. Emma's brother, the former manager of the second trekking company, Happy Trails, has himself moved to England after marrying a British backpacker. Yulan Pancake House, recommended by *Lonely Planet*, features banana pancakes and milkshakes, as well as the more enigmatic "Israeli fried

FIG. 14. *Postcards on the wall at Emma's Kitchen, Songpan. Note Princess Diana. Photo by author.*

noodles." Both offer addresses of backpackers' hostels in Chengdu. Unlike restaurants at Jiuzhaigou, they are local family enterprises.

Having been left officially "undeveloped," while in fact quietly growing a tourist industry oriented towards Western backpackers outside the pale of tourism authorities and corporations, the town had, to us, an intimate, harmonious feel that scenic spots and official "old towns," not to mention new developments like Chuanzhusi, lacked. The zone inside the old city gates was a living part of the town; it functioned as a pedestrian street where locals stroll leisurely (fig. 15). At night, the area was lit by yellow streetlights, rarely seen in Chinese cities, where neon tends to predominate. Here, there were no neon signs at all inside the gate, although the tower on the gate itself was illuminated with colorful lights. Unlike other gates in cities that had been developed into scenic spots, such as Nanjing, this one had no fence or ticket; locals sat and smoked on the wide terrace of the tower. Although the businesses on the main street of the old town, selling Tibetan clothes, curios, and yak meat to tourists, employ an increasing share of the locals (with more finding jobs in Chuanzhusi and Jiuzhaigou), agriculture is still an important part of

FIG. 15. *Strollers at the North Gate of Songpan. Photo by author.*

the economy. So far, modernity has arrived here, at least in part, not by the diktat of tourism developers seeking to replicate "success models" elsewhere or the imagery of national media shows. It has taken a gentler shape that, like the milkshake made of yak milk because no cow's milk is available, feels at once more local and more global than scenic-spot fare. What is missing, by contrast, is a strong sense of the national.

Development Has No Room for the Local

Now that Songpan County has become the gateway for air passengers coming to the Ngawa region, the county government wants to "develop" Songpan too. The deputy head of the tourist bureau, established in 1990, told us about the bureau's vision of Songpan as a transit hub for tourists not just to Jiuzhaigou and Huanglong, but also to other attractions of "Greater Jiuzhai."[11] While Chuanzhusi remains the main focus of development, there are plans to develop five scenic areas, as well as a Tibetan scenic village with "cultural activities," in the county (existing scenic spots, in addition to Huanglong, include Mounigou, a smaller reserve, and the Long March Memorial). These

FIGS. 16A and 16B. Demolished house and plan of the new square in front of the North Gate of Songpan. Photos by author.

scenic spots, as well as "National Flirtatious Expressions" of the Tibetans, Qiang, and Hui, are features of the tourist bureau's new promotional brochure; Songpan itself functions only as a backdrop.

Nonetheless, making tourists spend more time in the county involves a long-term project of reviving Songpan's old town. The town's homegrown infrastructure does not figure in development plans. The recently approved master plan (*guihua*) envisages raising the town wall to its original height and "rebuilding"—on the basis of old pictures and historical records—"Ming- and Qing-era houses" inside the walled town in place of the two- and three-story concrete-and-tile houses and older wooden houses that currently occupy the area. Residents are to be moved out into a new residential district. These plans have been approved despite the fact that the walled town, in its current state, has been declared a provincial-level cultural protection unit. Tourism officials reason that they want the old town to be an enclosed area for tourists only, like Lijiang in Yunnan or Pingyao in Shanxi. While—as we have seen in the water towns around Shanghai—such an arrangement is common for "old towns" that have been "developed" for tourism, the officials see Lijiang and Pingyao as models because both have been recognized as part of UNESCO's World Cultural Heritage. The deputy head believes that Songpan, too, will have a chance to apply for the status if the new buildings in the walled town are demolished and the "old" ones are "rebuilt." So far, however, it is the old wooden houses leaning on the outside of the town wall that are being demolished (fig 16a). At the North Gate, a large poster depicts the planned development: a renovated town wall and a new, modern square in front of the gate (fig. 16b).[12]

Scenic Spots: Sources of Authority

What are the sources of cultural authority that enshrine scenic spots?

Delimitation and Development

First of all, to qualify as such, they have to be delimited and "developed" (*kaifa*) or "constructed" (*jianshe*), terms of the Chinese Communist newspeak that were invented in high "socialism" but now denote commercialization rather than industrialization. As an official of the Anhui Province Tourism Bureau writes, "traditional routes should be subjected to scientific selection, a few of the most unique and promising routes must be chosen and developed profoundly" (Zhang Yongxian 1991:29). For instance, Qiao Yu, director of the Badaling Special Zone within the municipality of Beijing—the place most tourists go to when they visit the Great Wall—writes in *Tourism Tribune*:[13]

Building Badaling Great Wall into a museum-like scenic spot . . . is strengthen-ing the [b]uilding environment and creating cultural and historic atmosphere . . . integrating with sightseeing, cultural display, academic research, historic and patriotic education. (Qiao 2001:43)[14]

The authors of a 1999 book entitled *Megatrends of Chinese Tourism Development in the New Century (Zhongguo Lüyouye Xin Shiji Fazhan Da Qushi)* describe a suc-cessful case of "development" in the *hutongs* (alleys lined with traditional walled residences with inside courts) of Beijing:

Twenty years ago, everybody thought these *hutongs* had very high cultural
content [*wenhua hanliang*], that they were one of the best tourism resources
in Beijing, but for so many years, this was limited to talk. It seemed like a
good resource, a superior resource, but it was not turned into a product. Then,
Beijing established the Hutong Cultural Development Company and recruited
two hundred migrant workers, organized dozens of rickshaws, standardized
equipment, designed routes, putting the resources of the *hutong* to real use.
(Wei et al. 1999:14)

This agenda, of course, reflects a view of tourism as a means of mod-ernization and "civilization." This is particularly true in areas inhabited by "backward" ethnic "minorities" (Gang Xu 1999; Oakes 1998:126–57). Indeed, as an official explained to Oakes, villagers "don't understand how to develop tourism. . . . If they open their village by themselves it will be a mess. . . . They'll have to wait for us to do it for them" (Oakes 1998:184). The official's vision of development was as follows: "you buy a ticket, you go in and you get to see all sorts of activities, song and dance performances, at any time. When we open Huashishao it will be like [the China Folk Culture Villages in] Shenzhen" (ibid.). When Xu Xinjian visited the First Village of the West-ern Qiang in Ngawa, he was pleasantly surprised at the absence of the "mov-ing pictures" promised in the promotional materials; he "regarded the tranquility that had somehow survived the forces of tourism as unusual" (Xu 2001:205). But a county tourism official, originally from that very village, was dissatisfied that "the village was far from meeting the goal of tourism exploitation set out for it mainly because the local people were not interested and lacked ability" (ibid.). Thus according to both officials, locals could be used as a resource, but in strictly regimented fashion. Their interaction with tourists had to be controlled, lest they subvert development.

For these officials, "developing" a tourist village meant undertaking what the leisure business terms "theming": creating a "tourist product" with a clear narrative of meaning, supported by a multitude of performative and interactive features—displays, shows, and visitor activities. This can be seen as a response to the popularity of theme parks, which often provide formative experiences for Chinese tourists and tourism entrepreneurs, but as we have seen, it is also related to the historical memory of Chinese travel. In any case, the similarity of the experience of visiting a scenic spot to visiting a theme park helps explain why theme parks are themselves seen as scenic spots. It also explains why development focuses exclusively on the scenic spot itself: whatever is outside its boundaries, along the route, does not count. "There is nothing special here for tourists"—literally, "there is nothing really tourable here" (zheli mei shenme hao lüyou de)—is a comment I often heard when I asked residents outside scenic spots for their recommendations of what to see. The use of the word lüyou, travel or tour, as a transitive verb implies that it is understood as being directed at objects—in this case, sites.

The paradoxes of this type of development have been pointed out by Oakes in his study of rural ethnic tourism. "Tourist villages" are supposed to represent the "primitive" against which the urban tourist can define his or her modernity. Yet at the same time, the idea of "development" follows models based on what an "ethnic" village or performance must be like in "modern" media and theme park representations, driven partly by "ethnic" villagers who return home from working at theme parks with the desire to appropriate the commercial success of the parks (Oakes 1998:182). Xu Xinjian (2001:207–8) describes a young woman who began using her native village as a resource after she became a county tourism official: she instructed her family members to "put on a traditional 'ethnic' aspect of simple primitivism," wear ethnic costumes, and dance.

Classification and Endorsement

Second, scenic spots have to be classified and approved by a legal or cultural authority (fig. 17).

FIG. 17. *The stele declaring Huanglong's status as a World Heritage Site is itself a tourist attraction. Photo by author.*

The ranking of scenic spots goes back to the literati tradition: as early as 1170, the *Notes on a Journey to Shu* (*Ru shu ji*) of the famous poet-official Lu You cited the since-lost *Ranking of Waters* in claiming that a spring Lu visited in modern Sichuan was the "Fourth Finest Spring in the World" (Strassberg 1994:211). Since 1982, various state bodies—partly to compete with each other—have maintained and periodically updated numerous lists of sites. In 1998, these included 119 National Key Scenic Areas (introduced in 1982), 750 National Key Cultural Relics Protection Units, and 99 Historic and Cultural Cities of National Fame (China Cultural Relics Research Association et al. 1998:393–411). In 2004, there were already 177 National Key Scenic Areas, and parallel classifications of "tourist scenic spots" (*lüyou jingqu*)—with the top category designated "national AAAA level"—and of "superior tourist cities" (*youxiu lüyou chengshi*) had appeared (of the latter, there were fifty-four in 2003). In addition, there are National Sites of Patriotic Education and National Model Sites for Civilized Scenic and Tourist Areas (*quanguo wenming lüyou fengjingqu shifandian*). All of the above classifications also exist at provincial, prefectural, and county levels. Finally, since 1987, UNESCO has approved around thirty World Natural and Cultural Heritage Sites in China. Placement on the UNESCO list has become the most coveted classification, as World Heritage sites are seen as "world-class scenic spots" that should serve as "models for the whole business" (Wei et al. 1999:18). UNESCO's 1998 monitoring report on Jiuzhaigou noted (with satisfaction rather than irony) the comments of the site's management that "since the site was designated as World Heritage . . . 'the mountains are greener, the lakes bluer and the people more handsome'!" (Thorsell 2004). The designation is the subject of intense competition between local and provincial governments, since every national government is only allowed one application per year. "We want to convince UNESCO that it is not fair," said Miao Yuyan, the director of the Tourism Administration of Sichuan, one of the provinces with the most UNESCO sites; "China is so big, and it should be allowed more applications than small countries like those in Europe."[15]

These classifications are displayed on brass tablets at the gates of the sites and on tickets and brochures, and they appear in guidebooks and other travel publications, with an obvious impact on the canon of mingsheng. They also convey a sense of constant competition between scenic spots, both nationally and internationally. For instance, a "Tourist Itinerary Map of Hebei Province" published by the Hebei Tourist Administration contains the following information (in English):

There are 542 cultural relics in the province. Among them, 58 are directly under state protection and 2 are awarded World Cultural Heritage by UN.
In addition, the province has 4 national historic cities, 3 "Forty topping views of the country," 5 national scenic areas, 8 national forests and 3 national nature reserves. In recent years, Hebei tourism has developed rapidly. Now it boasts 432 scenic spots, 20 provincial holiday villages, 165 star-rated hotels and 370 travel services. . . . This year Hebei promotes 8 tourist routes.

One of the latest ranking initiatives was the government-organized competition of mountains. Ten out of the forty-two competing mountains, including Mount Tai and Mount Everest, received award letters and plaques (Travel.ru, February 5, 2003). Formal ranking is part of a broader attempt to rate objects of nature and architecture according to an "objective" and universal system of reference: "the biggest Buddha statue," "the oldest bridge," "the world-famous canal," or "the most secluded mountain under

FIG. 18. Entry ticket to the "old town" of Zhouzhuang, Jiangsu. Sites visited are ticked off on the right. Author's collection.

heaven." At the same time, promotional literature is rich in traditional four-character superlatives that resound with the cultural authority of classical Chinese, such as "lofty and awe-inspiring," "grand and fantastic," and "splendid and imposing." These epithets are chosen to describe certain kinds of sites not at random but following an established standard with which all writers are familiar.

Serialization

Third, scenic spots are constructed as a series of attractions: natural formations, statues, archaeological relics, or simply views (fig. 18). The series—and generally the order of viewing—is standard and is reproduced, mostly identically, in guide narratives, visitors' brochures, and guidebooks. This kind of serialization is different from, but rhymes with, Benedict Anderson's idea of seriality as a logic underlying nation building (Anderson 1998).

Standardization and Commodification

Fourth, a visit to a scenic spot—whether a canyon, a temple, a Red Army monument, or an amusement park—should fulfill expectations for what tourists generally do, which is most commonly described as *wan*, literally, "playing" or entertaining oneself. It follows that sites share much of their design, from tickets and ticket booths to the use of space, the schedule and choreography of visits and song-dance performances, the souvenir shops and restaurants along the main street, and hotel lobbies. Equally alike are the phrases used on explanatory signs, in brochures, and by tour guides, as well as the music coming out of the loudspeakers. Inscribed steles stand at photo spots in "pristine" Jiuzhaigou, and a "forest" of inscribed steles has been erected near Mao's birthplace to recall the "stele forests" at *mingsheng* such as Mount Tai, the ancient capital of Xi'an, or Guilin. Tour guides carrying identical banners lead tour participants wearing uniform baseball caps, whose contact with locals is limited to a few dialogic situations replicated from site to site. The uniqueness of the site, like that of Tibetan and Qiang songs in the Jiuzhaigou performance, does not have to come from the experience; it is enough simply to be told about it. The hotels, the beer, and the songs may look, taste, and sound the same, but they are named after Shangri-La in the eponymous county, the Sani goddess Ashima in the Stone Forest, and Chairman Mao in his hometown. In fact, this "branding" process may be contributing to shifts in ethnic identities: Xu Xinjian describes successful cases of tourism-induced construction of ethnic labels of small local groups based on "distinctive" ritual and drama performances (2001:197–98).

Commercialization is not only rapid and uniform—in Lijiang County (population 63,000), there are 160 hotels, 180 jade shops, and 900 guides (Duang 2000:24; Peters 2001:323), and in the "water town" of Zhouzhuang (population 5,000), there are over 500 shops and restaurants (Becker 2004)—but also strikingly overt. Unlike tourism development in the West, no attempts are made to disguise commercialization through clever design, use of materials, or sales behavior. Ticket gates and service stations abound. Western tourists desirous of an "authentic" or "picturesque" shot, purified of blatant signs of tourist activity, look around in desperation. The result of such uniform and self-conscious commercialization is the erasure of differences between tourist practices that, in the West, are perceived as distinct, such as ecotourism versus sightseeing.[16]

Since the site is perceived as a product, it makes sense that it should have clear boundaries, cost money to access, and have instructions according to which it should best be consumed. It makes sense that its quality be rated, approved, and ranked, and that it should be designed and constructed according to the latest advances in the field. Apart from providing a cultural master narrative of the site, disco-infused "ethnic" performances serve to convey a self-conscious experience of tourism as modern consumption to both the tourist and, as Oakes points out, the local who provides the entertainment;

it does not, for its marketers or consumers, invalidate the "ethnic" essence or the special nature of the show.

National Enclaves

Scenic spots in China are what Tim Edensor calls "enclavic tourist spaces" (Edensor 1998:45). Based on his fieldwork at the Taj Mahal in India, Edensor describes such spaces as being created for the exclusive use of Westerners: "They provide no facilities available for locals' use, nor spaces in which they may wander, socialize or linger. Locals may spend their work-time there, but rarely their leisure time" (47). Instead, domestic tourists predominate in "heterogeneous tourist spaces," which "accommodate tourism . . . but are not dominated by it" (54) and are not subject to special regulations. Such spaces are also preferred by alternative Western tourists, such as backpackers (149–80).

This scheme, which Edensor extends to "developing countries" in general, reflects the tendency of tourism research to regard "locals" as either immobile or, as in Edensor's case, mobile in some different, pre-modern, pre-commercial way—like pilgrims, for example. Because he sees tourist enclaves as spaces not catering to locals, Edensor, quoting Goffmann's description of a "total institution," posits that, like theme parks, enclaves are "cut off from the wider society," unrelated to vernacular constructions of the society that surrounds them (Edensor 1998:49). Yet in China, "enclavic" spaces are clearly designed for and dominated by domestic tourists and are firmly part of the national context. Contrary to Edensor's view, these enclaves are *both* theme parks and educational institutions for citizens.

By contrast, the development of "heterogeneous" spaces—such as Songpan—is driven primarily by the needs of Western backpackers, who tend to be disappointed with scenic spots, which they perceive as inauthentic, unromantic, boring, and tacky. For *Lonely Planet*, the backpacker bible that appears to have played a part in the emergence of Songpan and other towns in China and Vietnam as backpacker destinations (Peters 2001:329), Chinese-style tourist development is definitely bad news. "Unfortunately, Zhouzhuang has been given the dreaded Chinese tourism make-over," laments *Lonely Planet Shanghai*, going on to warn of the "blight of tacky tourist amenities" in Hangzhou (Mayhew 2004:169, 179). (Similarly, *Lonely Planet Vietnam* describes Dalat, a popular domestic tourist destination, as "the Disneyland of the central high-

lands" and "the final word in Vietnamese kitsch" [quoted in Alneng 2002:132].)
Lijiang, which started out as a backpacker destination but was later turned
into a scenic spot, still gets many backpackers, but an English backpacker
we met in Songpan told us that she thought "Lijiang is a bit of a trap, and I
don't like old Chinese architecture anyway." Two Dutch backpackers said they
had skipped Lijiang deliberately. *Rough Guide China* berates Lijiang for its "fake
architecture" "displayed like in a cultural theme park," and for pretending
to be "ethnic" while it was "really completely Han." In Songpan, the Thai and
Dutch organizers of a group of Dutch adventure tourists presented a nostalgic and negative narrative of Chinese tourism development, blaming
Chinese tourists for "spoiling" northern Sichuan. They had been coming to
Songpan since the mid-1990s: at that time, it had been all wooden houses,
"beautiful," but now Chinese tourism development had built it up because
"it's old; we don't like it; we need modern." With the construction of an asphalt
road between Ngawa and Gansu, it was increasingly difficult to find "real
nomads." Now Chinese groups from Jiuzhaigou went there; they descended
from their buses, had a tea, took a photo on a yak, and drove back. By contrast, when the Dutch went there, they "tried to talk to the nomads in their
tents." An article in the left-liberal British newspaper *Independent*, entitled
"Faking it: Chinese burn their bridges with the past," lambasted Zhouzhuang
as a "national scandal." "Closer inspection reveals," the author wrote about
Tongli, a neighboring "water town," with a clear sense of deception, "that
the most attractive and picturesque old buildings are modern fakes" (Becker
2004). A Spanish tourist, quoted in another article, said, "I think we search
more for something original and more authentic, and they [Chinese tourists]
just look for something nice and clean and bright" (Lim 2004).

Tourism service providers specializing in serving Western backpackers
have adapted to this view, which values little-traveled routes and simplicity
and which distances itself from Chinese tourism. When we asked Emma, of
Emma's Café in Songpan, about a particular route, she answered that it was
"beautiful, but there are many Chinese tourists." Tourism officials in some
regions that are poor in scenic spots and rely mainly on Western adventure
tourism—and use them as arbiters of touristic modernity—have also adopted
this view: they see the performative "ethnic villages" as "inauthentic" and
are critical of Chinese tourists. As the director of the Southeast Guizhou Travel
Bureau, specializing in "ethnic villages," told Oakes, "Chinese are only interested in staying in big fancy hotels, seeing famous scenic spots" (Oakes
1998:173). He, on the other hand, "was increasingly convinced that the most

authentic understanding of village culture came through spontaneous inter-action and discovery" (175)—tropes central to the "romantic gaze" of the Western tourist—and protested that his prefecture was "not a theme park . . . *it's the real thing*" (182). Chinese researchers of tourism with international experience, including prominent ones associated with the National Tour-ism Administration (CNTA), also take sharply critical views of "destructive development" and "overbuilding" and stress the need to preserve local cul-ture while introducing international standards of infrastructure. Thus, Wei Xiaoan, a former CNTA department head, explained that he would never sup-port the construction of a hotel in a village in the Dong ethnic area of Guizhou Province. Still, he revealed the ambivalence of his position by adding that he had supported a local village head's initiative to build a drum tower. The vil-lage head had argued that the tower was "our own" culture, and that all other villages had it, "only we don't."[17]

3

MAKING SENSE OF SCENIC SPOTS

Encasement and uniformity are prominent features of tourism development in China. These are related to the revival of pre-modern representations of *mingsheng*, which is in turn facilitated by China's lack of the distinctly modern, romantic, exploratory, and self-bettering discourses of tourism that emerged in the West after the Enlightenment. In late socialist China, the notion of the scenic spot has been appropriated by the state's nation-building project and has become hegemonic in the tourism market due to the state's high degree of direct and indirect economic and political control of that sector.

Literati Versus Bourgeois Travel

Postmodernist authors in the first half of the nineties have argued that the pursuit of authenticity, the "romantic gaze," is no longer decisive in Western tourism. The tourist, they said, is increasingly either unconcerned with "the substitution of originals with facsimiles . . . so long as the expected narrative is sustained" (Diller + Scofidio 1994:39) or—enter the "post-tourist"—realizes the self-defeating nature of the pursuit, is aware of what MacCannell identified as the "staged" nature of tourist attractions, and is consciously, though perhaps ironically, engaged in the play at authenticity. Perhaps the strongest argument in favor of this view was presented by architects Diller + Scofidio in their 1994 exhibition in Caen, "Suitcase Studies: The Production of a National Past." Each of the fifty "suitcase studies" presented an American tourist site dedicated to a person or event important in the construction of America's national past. As in China, the significance of most of these sites is attested by the state: they are state monuments, state historic sites, or national military parks. Many employ staff dressed in period costume—and in one case, even trained to speak the purported English of the Puritans. The houses of several historical personalities, such as "Theodore Roosevelt's Birthplace," are actually replicas, while many battlefields feature regular costumed reenactments of historical battles. Henry Ford's Greenfield Village in Michigan is a theme park of American history featuring buildings from Edison's laboratory to Lincoln's law office. Diller and Scofidio's take on American tourism is much like mine on Chinese tourism, except that they portray tourism as a conscious game between producers and tourists, "a tacit pact of semi-fiction between sightseers and sightmakers which results in a highly structured yet delirious free play of space-time which thwarts simple, binary distinctions between the real and the counterfeit" (Diller + Scofidio 1994:52). In this process, "a sight must struggle to resemble its expected image," which is defined by "the 'official' set of views," i.e., the hegemonic representation circulated in the media (43). According to Diller and Scofidio:

The touristic construction puts into motion an exchange of references between a sight and its indispensable components—the postcard, the plaque, the marker, the brochure, the guided tour, the souvenir, the snapshot, and further, the replica, the reenactment, etc. . . . [A] tourist sight can be considered to be only *one* of its many representations, thus eliminating the "dialectics of authenticity" altogether. (1994:45, emphasis in original)

This perspective is analytically useful because it questions the pervasive dichotomy between "bad" mass tourism and "good" individual travel, between the homogeneity of the inauthentic "staged attraction" and the diversity of authentic "culture." Yet it is precisely the pervasiveness of such moral notions—which govern the travel choices and reactions of so many Western tourists and which have arguably kept tourism at the margins of social studies, as something peripheral to "serious" social processes—that makes it impossible to reduce their pursuit to a game and declare the demise of the "romantic gaze." For example, a recent editorial in the travel supplement of the French newspaper *Le Nouvel Observateur*—which also carried advertisements for package tours and cruises—read:

In the year 2000, mass tourism has served its time. We dream of travel as an individual accomplishment, but one with an ethical concern. . . . In the year 2000, we scrutinize ourselves for a tourism that is respectful of the other. . . . In the year 2000, we are concerned with ecology. (MIT 2002:25)

The editorial expresses the latest embodiment of Western tourism's built-in guilt complex: the movement known within the tourism industry as New Tourism, which aims for more differentiation, individualization, and cultural and environmental "awareness" in the marketing of holidays (Butcher 2003:7). The editorial is quoted in a critical collection of French papers on tourism, which observes that "the consensus is . . . that the intellectual must at least view [tourism] critically, that is, with suspicion." Why, it asks, "do we accept so commonly a discourse of rejection of the other?" (MIT 2002:5).

Enlightenment, Embourgeoisement, and the Shaping of the Tourist in Europe

Marc Boyer has written that "the touristic revolution was simultaneous to all the other revolutions that characterized the progress of Great Britain in the 18th century" (1999:3). More generally, the conventions and values of modern Western travel are closely linked to the experiences of the Enlightenment and nineteenth-century industrialization. From the end of the eighteenth century, travelers no longer wanted picturesque, artistically arranged landscapes; as the first American wilderness painter, British-born Thomas Cole, wrote, "no Tivolis, no Ternis, Mont Blancs, Plinlimmons, hackneyed and worn by the daily pencils of hundreds, but virgin forests, lakes and waterfalls" (cited in Löfgren 1999:47). As tourism began to emerge as an accepted element of bourgeois culture in the nineteenth century, it was shaped by a number of new sensibilities: the romantic cult of the sublime, to be found in the untamed wilderness; the positivistic appeal of exploring nature and culture; the fashionable image of the urban *flâneur*; and somewhat later, the self-bettering, educational, mass-mobilizing zeal of the nationalist and labor tourist-excursionist movements. Early on, these sensibilities defined what John Urry (1990) calls the "romantic gaze" of the tourist: the quest for an "authentic" travel experience, one focused on untouched, untouristed places as opposed to "inauthentic" mass tourism. The image of the tourist has been associated with "the beaten track" and with the "tourist trap" ever since tourism as a concept emerged. Writing in 1792, Adam Walker criticized the "rattling tourist" for "exciting envy and false ideas of happiness among the peaceful inhabitants" (quoted in Ousby 1990:15); a century later, W. H. Mallock reaffirmed that "the true traveler seeks precisely what the excursionist dreads" (quoted in Buzard 1993:8). The opposition of the "good traveler" to the "bad tourist" was reinforced in the entire canon of belles-lettres that came to be associated with tourism, from Wordsworth through Dickens, Mark Twain, E. M. Forster, Henry James and Ruskin, to Virginia Woolf, D. H. Lawrence, Evelyn Waugh, T. S. Eliot, and W. H. Auden, or, to mention a non-English writer, Hans Magnus Enzensberger. James Buzard sums up his literary history of the "anti-tourist" in Waugh's famous phrase: "The tourist is the other fellow" (Buzard 1993:1).

As nineteenth-century organizers of package tours made travel possible for the middle and even working classes, they were acutely aware of the stigma of mass travel and attempted to deny the corollary charges of standardization and poor taste. They took their cue from Thomas Cook, who affirmed in 1854 that "Taste and Genius may look out of third-class windows" (quoted in Buzard 1993:51). The more tourists were accused of falling for the inauthentic, the more vigilant they became. According to Mandler, "the common Victorian tourist was not only *able* to distinguish, but frequently angrily defended the age value of historic buildings against modern vandals" (Mandler 1999:137–38). As early as the 1840s, popular magazines claimed best-known buildings as national possessions, which not even their owners had the right to modernize (ibid). At the same time, the desire of tourists—influenced by their literary models— to not be "mere tourists" produced an emphasis on individuality in travel that propelled the use of guidebooks, which, as Karl Baedeker wrote in 1858, were intended to help the traveler "break free of 'the unpleasant . . . tutelage of hired servants and guides[,] . . . to render him *independent*'" (quoted in Buzard 1993:75). In the ethos of the guidebooks, individualism went hand in hand with a critical view on consumerism (Koshar 2000:45). Because tourism is supposed to be the antipode to the commercialization of modern life, fear of and equivocation about the commercial has always been its constitutive element. Post-colonial and ecological guilt—fueled by the bulk of "first-world" studies on tourism in the "Third World"—has more recently added one more stigma to being a tourist (MIT 2002:68).

The Socialist Tourist in China and the Soviet Union: The Pocket Tourism Encyclopedia *(Beijing, 1988) and* The Tourist's Concise Handbook *(Moscow, 1985)*

In the late nineteenth and early twentieth centuries, Russia shared these discourses with Western Europe. On the eve of World War I, it had a reasonably well-developed network of travel agents, a range of guidebooks, and a significant, in part social democratic educational tourist-excursionist movement (McReynolds 2003:164–71; Usyskin 2000:74; Ely 2003). It is this latter aspect of tourism that the Soviet government chose to put into its service—as late as the early 1930s still explicitly relating to the "proletarian tourism" of Weimar Germany (Sandomirskaya 1998)—while at the same time severely curbing sightseeing tourism, whether foreign or domestic, organized or individual.

In terms of mass impact, the ideology of tourism as a tool of mobilization, education, and self-betterment, and to some extent as planned leisure, was less important for Soviet life than the similarly conceived but more successfully executed Dopolavoro movement for Fascist Italy or Kraft durch Freude for Nazi Germany. On the other hand, it had a much longer-lasting effect on the understanding of what tourism was. Although organized sightseeing "excursions" existed, "tourism" (*turizm*) essentially came to mean "amateur" (*samodeyatel'nyi*) tourism: self-catered tent-dwelling treks, kayak tours, and mountain climbs by rugged, steeled (*zakalennye*) men and women, perhaps in pursuit of the Tourist of the USSR pin or Master of Sports in Tourism degree. The parallel notion of "rest" or "recreation" (*otdykh*)—also shared with Nazism and Fascism—meant state-assigned vouchers (*putevki*) to state-owned rest houses (*doma otdykha*) or sanatoria, with a regimen somewhere between a resort and a hospital (see Koenker 2003; Gorsuch 2003).

In China, by contrast, neither the Communists nor their pre-1949 nationalist or liberal rivals picked up on modern bourgeois ideas of travel and tourism. The tourist as self-educating fighter for nation or class was as much missing from the Chinese discourse as was the romantic tourist or the explorer. Though a culture of urban *flânerie* attained a certain development in pre–World War II Shanghai, bourgeois tourist practices as such did not catch on widely. Whereas Russian travel agents had operated since 1867 (McReynolds 2003:166), the first Chinese travel agency opened in 1927 and had only a few customers every year before the war forced it to close (Qian 2003:145).

The ideals of pre-modern, pre-commercial literati travel and of *mingsheng* continued to dominate the idea of travel, and once the ideological and practical constraints on leisure travel were loosened, those ideals resurfaced within the context of post-1978 modernization and an emerging consumer culture. To the extent that Soviet-style "rest houses" and sanatoria (*liaoyangyuan*) had existed during the preceding period—albeit accessible only to a narrow elite—they were now associated with Mao-era practices and doomed to oblivion. Instead, self-help literature on tourism in the 1980s instructed Chinese readers not only about visiting *mingsheng* but also about being consumers on the road. *The Pocket Tourism Encyclopedia* (Lüyou xiaobaike), like other similar works, gives short introductions to all National Key Scenic Areas, Historic and Cultural Cities of National Fame, and National Key Cultural Protection Units, as well as its own selection of theme, amusement, and other parks. But in addition, it provides answers to questions such as "How to hire a taxi" (Shandong 1988:190) and "How to use the equipment of an airplane seat" (201) and contains similarly didactic sections on hotels (206–11), on souvenir shopping (211–32), and on "typical local products" (*fengwei techan*, 233–56). This is supplemented with a list of major Western hotel chains and tourism organizations.

All this information was, at the time, of purely theoretical value for most readers: the encyclopedia recommended readers to use boats, meaning that a trip from Shanghai to Dalian, for example, would have taken weeks in a country with almost no holidays. But it was clearly intended to shape the way fledgling tourists behaved, and it prepared future tourists for the late 1990s campaigns equating "leisure culture" with consumption. These expectations were in stark contrast to those of *The Tourist's Concise Handbook* (Kratkii spravochnik turista) published in Moscow three years earlier (Shtyurmer 1985). This book is all about outdoors techniques, from how to make a backpack to how to choose a campsite. In addition, it contains the rules for obtaining sports titles (*razryady*) (24–25) and for performing "socially useful work" (226). The Chinese book, typical of books of its time, defined tourism as "travel for the purposes of holidaymaking, cures (*liaoyang*), sightseeing, visiting friends, inspection (*kaocha*) and knowledge-seeking" (Shandong 1988:1) and portrayed it as a phenomenon of modern consumption: "In America and other Western countries, people have become used to hopping on airplanes on weekends or traveling in individual cars. This shows that . . . tourism is closely linked to the results of modern social development" (4–5). For the Russian author, tourism is the kind of active leisure and wellness of laborers with the strongest mass character, one of the important means of education of the Soviet people. . . . Correctly organized and conducted amateur tourist travel ensures good . . . physical development of tourists . . . [and] teaches them collectivism, love of nature, discipline, courage, and initiative. (Shtyurmer 1985:3)

While this author does not refer to Western tourism at all, he nonetheless implicitly differentiates Soviet tourism from "bourgeois tourism," which consists of mere "entertainment" and the "pursuit of the unusual," a distinction made explicitly by earlier Soviet authors (see Gorsuch 2003:779).

The two books do not overlap: the Soviet one says nothing about sightseeing, and the Chinese one keeps silent on trekking or camping. Although both the Soviet and Chinese projects acknowledge that tourism is a tool of "patriotic education" (Shtyurmer 1985:226; Shandong 1988:495), the Soviet approach sees the means of that education mainly in the correct way of being a tourist, regardless of where tourism takes place. (Even though excursions to revolutionary or war battle sites were also organized in the Soviet Union, they were marginal to the discourse of tourism.) In the Chinese approach, by contrast, the means of patriotic education lies entirely in the acceptance of pre-defined interpretations of particular sites through the act of consuming them. For the *Pocket Encyclopedia*, the good tourist is not one who is rugged and selfless (as in the Soviet discourse), nor one who recognizes the authentic and approaches it in an authentic way (as in the Western discourse), but one who *learns the canonical representations of the sites he is planning to visit.* The book urges the readers to avoid the

often seen phenomenon in tourism that, traveling through the Three Gorges, one sees the beautiful Goddess Peak but does not know the moving story of "the immortal woman facing her spouse"; one tours the Bitao Well at the River-Watching Pavilion Park in Chengdu but does not know the facts about Bitao and that she used the well's water to make ink to present (a poem) to her pen-friend. (Shandong 1988:141)

Without such knowledge, the author warns, tourists might feel disappointed ("indignant") about the decrepitude of the sights.

However, it is not quite enough to simply learn the appropriate cultural references attached to scenic spots. In addition, one is expected to take photos of them, a subject to which a chapter of the book is devoted. The emphasis here is as much on teaching readers the proper content of the photos as it is on the technical skills of taking them. Each site, or at least each type of site, should be represented by elements that have been recognized as its essence.

Each famous mountain and great river has its specifics. Mount Tai is heroic; Huashan is dangerous; the Yellow River is turbid (heroic); the Li River is clear (brilliant). Visiting a place . . . one should pay detailed attention to what angle of photography can bring out the representative, typical photo.

When photographing famous mountains and great rivers, one must always pay attention to buildings of historical relic value and of local color. For example, the Tilted Bridge on the Yellow River, the "guest-welcoming pines" on Huang-shan and the like. (Shandong 1988:493–94)

Do not let objects unrelated to the theme interfere with your frame. For example, when taking the picture of a person at Mt. Tai—the Mountain of the East—green pines, lofty rocks . . . can be said to be related to the theme, while pipes carrying water to the mountain, signs of vending stalls etc. are considered unrelated to the theme. (ibid.:491)

As much as possible, choose photographs of interesting mingsheng and ancient relics. For example, taking a picture of Yueyang Pavilion (on the Yangzi) can make people think about the . . . ancient quatrains; taking a picture at the Yue Temple in Hangzhou can conjure up people's admiration for the national hero, Yue Fei, and their contempt for the shameless traitors. (ibid.:498)

The prospective tourist is even initiated into the intricacies of which strand of the narrative of the national past to choose if there are several possibilities at a given site:

Capture the key shot (guanjian sheying) of a mingsheng or ancient relic. For example, the Gold Mountain Temple in Zhenjiang is famous for the beautiful legend of the white maiden; the camera can focus on the view of meeting at the "severed bridge." . . . For another, at Sun Yatsen's Mausoleum in Nanjing, taking a picture of the thousand steps carved in stone, symbolizing Sun Yatsen's untiring, lifelong struggle for country and people, is preferable to taking a picture of the heroic and imposing architecture. (Shandong 1988:498)

Although the images of particular "minorities" were not yet fully developed in the 1980s, there were nonetheless proper ways to photograph local customs (*fengtu renqing*). Photos were to reflect "the attitude of the healthy and optimistic observer; photographing the backward, unsanitary, or impoverished should be resolutely avoided" (Shandong 1988:494). While Soviet tourists were still supposed to be masculinizing themselves, Chinese tourists were being instructed in feminizing the other.

Learning to reproduce the correct representation of a site is important: at stake is one's ability "to express the infinity of one's feelings towards the rivers and mountains of the Fatherland": "only having mastered the skills and rules" of photography "can one get better at expressing these feelings" (Shandong 1988:495).

Finally, the book defines the role of the tour guide. Here, the stress is on the guide's narrative, which is supposed to "reflect objective facts," yet, contradictorily, also "express approval or disapproval, praise or opposition, pleasure and contempt." It is to be "continuous and uninterrupted, like the flow of clouds or water, with no glitch." The guide should master correct articulation and prosody and "use hyperboles, metaphors, similes" to ornament his speech. He should "turn the narrative into a story" by weaving into it fairy tales, legends, and stories of famous personalities related to the place (Shandong 1988:506–8). When viewing nature, the guide is to point out not only "usual views" of a mountain or a river, prominent through their natural features, but also "views that imitate shapes" (*xiang xing xing jingguan*)— such as the Goddess Peak in the Three Gorges—and "views that imitate sounds" (*xiang sheng xing jingguan*), such as the Lute Spring that sounds like a lute (516).

The Post-Socialist Reproduction of Literati Travel

There are alternatives to the tradition of literati travel in China. A tradition of introspective engagement with nature was strong in early imperial times, associated with Buddhist and Taoist ideals of the recluse and represented by widely known poets such as Xie Lingyun (385–443) and Wang Wei of the Tang. Their poetry projects an ideal of solitary seclusion in and union with nature (see Pauline Yu 1989). Like other aspects of Buddhist and Taoist thought, this "veneration of refuge and retreat" (Brook 1998:55) lived on in gentry travel in the late empire, and Cahill notes there are travel accounts, poetry, and paintings that express transcendent experiences of nature close to the European notion of the sublime. He adds, however, that this sort of response was not dominant and became increasingly uncommon in the late empire.[1] It has also been disprivileged in mainstream cultural discourse and education. On the other hand, much of the rural and urban population, particularly women, participated in pilgrimages, a well-developed and highly organized travel business during the late empire, separate from and disdained by the literati just as the "tourist" was disdained by eighteenth-century European writers (Wu 1992:74–78; see also the other chapters in Naquin and Yü 1992). But, though Chinese tourism today increasingly incorporates that tradition in practice, with tour guides adding incense-burning to their standard itineraries, there is no modern travel discourse akin to the Western traveler/tourist dichotomy to interpret it as a form of tourism. Tourists follow itineraries based on the signs of literati travel, but their traveling culture is more similar to that of the old pilgrims, with nothing to bridge the gap.

It is not that nature is more strongly culturalized in the Chinese literati tradition than in Europe—several authors (e.g., Ousby 1990; Löfgren 1999; Palmowski 2002) have shown that European nature tourism since the eighteenth century has been centered on landscapes associated with cultural heroes such as Wordsworth or Byron—but the Chinese tradition suggests a different way of approaching and responding to nature, lacking the modern Western taboo on human intervention. This is a tradition in which vast expanses of wilderness are tamed into a series of named cameo views, and harmony with nature, experienced in merry company with song and wine, serves to intensify feelings of affinity rather than introspection. The tickets, video clips, and "love locks" at Mount Emei are offensive for the Western tourist in search of "authenticity," since they appear incompatible with the historical and the sacred that constitute the very *raison d'être* of the tourist site. But seen in a different way, the experience is simply a technological improvement over the sedan chairs, entrance fees, and "post-summit receptions" that gentry travelers described encountering at Mount Tai in the seventeenth century (Wu 1992:74–75).

The responses of European middle-class travelers—whether early-twentieth-century Britons describing the Mont Blanc with Byronian phrases (Palmowski 2002:110) or contemporary visitors to the Louvre—were and are just as preconditioned by received information as those of Chinese literati, but the "romantic gaze" does not allow them, as "good" travelers, to acknowledge that fact; it demands that their experiences be authentic and therefore unique. Tourists who, as James Bryce wrote in 1865, "see the sights for no purpose but that of verifying their Murray (Guide)" (quoted in Buzard 1993:76) were satirized in numerous novels as early as Thackeray's 1851 *The*

Kickleberrys on the Rhine (ibid). It follows that the commodification of tourist sites has always had to be veiled. By contrast, the participatory nature of Chinese sightseeing (tourists are rarely "left alone to contemplate" as Wordsworth did in the Lake District, Byron in the Alps, or Goethe in front of Strassburg Cathedral), coupled with the positive value placed on "verifying" earlier accounts and the lack of the *flâneur* tradition, replicates the convivial, confirmatory, and destination-centered nature of literati voyages. Performance, not "everyday life," is expected and appreciated. Commodification of the sites is open and demonstrative and is generally seen as integral both to the modernization of the place and the country, as well as to the modern self. Demolition and rebuilding is not seen as offending the "cultural heritage." Several tourism surveys and articles note that Chinese tourists are less likely to complain about environmental degradation, littering, and overcrowding than Western tourists (see, e.g., Cater 2001:4167), and Hashimoto (2000) argues that this makes sense if a landscape is experienced not so much for "its own" sake as it is as a sign for a set of cultural references. Exiled Tibetan groups see cultural imperialism in the demolition of traditional Tibetan houses in Lhasa and the construction of modern concrete structures crudely painted "in the Tibetan style" (e.g., TIN 2002), yet the same is happening in other parts of China. What matters is not the date of the current construction, but that of the "original construction" (*shi jian*), and that is what tourist brochures provide.

Similarly, for the Western traveler, the local interlocutor—particularly in the role of the "native guide"—is valuable because he authenticates the experience of the place. For the Chinese tourist, there is no need for a "native guide." For him, as for the Westerner, the local is an object of contemplation and consumption; however, the local is not an interlocutor, since authentication of the experience comes from the professional tour guide, the travel agency, or the site management, as they are supposed to be more familiar with the cultural canon. Indeed, as an interlocutor, the local is suspicious and potentially threatening. Erik Cohen asserts that the professional guide, whose role is to interpret tourist attractions, faces the challenge of having to enshrine the site while convincing his audience of the attraction's authenticity, two objectives that are potentially contradictory (1985:26–27). In particular, "in the case of minor attractions . . . an elaborate enshrinement may be incongruent with the importance of the attraction, and hence impair its perceived authenticity" (Cohen 1985:27). In China, tourists may be suspicious of the enshrinement of a site and express doubt about whether the guide has led them to the right historical place, but the act of enshrinement does not appear to raise the problem of inauthenticity. Many villagers cooperate in the enshrinement or even initiate it, following models seen on television or at theme parks, making it more difficult for tourists to raise questions about authenticity.

Feeling the State in Tourism: Management and Pedagogy

The lack of a cultural tradition of valuing the wilderness may explain the tendency toward the encasement of nature into "scenic spots." But the sensory and narrative uniformity of tourist sites requires other explanations. One reason for this uniformity is the strong and continued involvement of the highly centralized Chinese state in defining tourism itineraries.

Historically, the development of both pilgrimage sites and literati *mingsheng* was influenced by imperial pilgrimages and the routes of the official courier. Of the Five Peaks upon which the most important imperial sacrifices were performed, Mounts Tai, Huashan, and Hengshan remain important scenic spots today. The *Scripture on History*, one of the earliest texts of the Confucian canon, traced the imperial sacrifices at Mount Tai to the mythical emperor Shun. Ever since the Qin emperor unified China, these sacrifices have been documented by officials in the imperial retinue. Ma Dibo's *Record of the Feng and Shan Sacrifices* from 56 C.E. is the first extant first-hand travel account by a Chinese author, and it influenced many later travel texts (Strassberg 1994:57–59). Prime Minister Li Peng, carving his inscription into Mount Tai in 1991, established himself as a successor both of the emperors and of the scholar-officials who left their inscriptions a thousand years earlier. These Tang and Song scholar-officials, whose inscriptions and accounts shaped the later canon of *mingsheng*, were mostly traveling on official business, and the Ming gentleman who undertook leisure travel used the road network of the official courier system even as he took advantage of the services of private tourism entrepreneurs.

The presence of the state in this history of travel is striking compared to Europe, where premodern states were too weak to play a comparable role. The rise of modern tourism in Europe, following the appearance of the railway and the steamship, was inextricable from the rise of the capitalist enterprise and "civil society." It is inseparable from the names of entrepreneurs such as Thomas Cook, Karl Baedeker, and John Murray, but also from the numerous "touring clubs" of hikers, yachtsmen, cyclists, and motorists, bourgeois or working-class institutions that sprang up from England to Russia in the nineteenth century and played an important role in the democratization of the social scene (see, e.g., McReynolds 2003:77–102).

In China, as we have seen, mass tourism emerged not as part of industrial modernization but as part of a state-led promotion of a service sector modeled after Western postindustrial consumer economies, at a time when the "modern citizen" was gradually being recast as consumer.[2] In the post-1978 era, the state chose to retain a defining presence in the tourism sector even as it proceeded to privatize the economy. This did not have to happen, and it did not happen in the other newly emerging tourist economy, Russia's. There, after the collapse of the Soviet Union in 1991, the development of new tourism began as a grassroots phenomenon. This tourism, first a trickle and then a burgeoning flow, was directed abroad, chiefly to Europe as well as to cheap beach holidays in Turkey and Egypt. From 1993 to 1994, the number of Russian tourists to the coastal region of Antalya in Turkey, for example, jumped twentyfold, from 3,500 to 66,000, according to the local tourism authority. Russian domestic tourism began to pick up again only after the devaluation of the ruble in 1998. Its development was influenced by the travel experiences Russians had gained abroad and driven by private travel agencies and local developers, although it remained tinted by Soviet ideals of "good tourism." As a result, both abroad and at home, what is called *ekstremalnyi turizm* or just *ekstrim* ("extreme tourism") has become very popular. This notion combines adventure and wilderness tourism and mountaineering with, for example, motorized beach sports such as jet skiing or parasailing.

By contrast, the possibilities for Chinese tourists to travel abroad remained much more severely constrained by both the exit policies of the Chinese government and the visa policies of destination countries. In addition, domestic travel in China remained much cheaper than travel abroad, which was not the case in Russia. Foreign travel experiences therefore had a very limited influence on the development and management of tourism in China. The literati tradition remained the only cultural model of travel to reach back to, but it provided few practical behavioral cues for the contemporary tourist. The detailed instructions of the *Concise Tourism Encyclopedia* had to be supplemented by the state's injunctions to "be civilized tourists" and to "insist on the 'Five Particulars and 'Four Beauties'" on the Jiuzhaigou ticket. For Chinese tourists, such exhortations are familiar, bearing a strong resemblance to the "civilization campaigns" against spitting, littering, cursing, and so on, but they do not constitute a specific code of "good tourist" behavior.

Tangible Presence: Administrative and Economic Control

Tourism development can be initiated by the local, the prefectural, the provincial or—rarely—the central government; by a business; or even by a journalist, but it can only take place with state approval and invariably involves some (usually local) government body as a stakeholder. This replicates the experience of theme park development: both Splendid China and China Folk Culture Villages were constructed by the state-owned China Travel Service together with its Hong Kong affiliate, China Travel International Investment Ltd. (Sofield and Li 1998:381).

Before 1998, government bodies participated in tourism development projects either directly or through a state-owned travel agency or other business. In 1998, responding in part to the price wars and fragmentation of the tourism market, the government announced a policy of "state withdrawal" from the management of tourism. The key result of that policy was, however, a series of acts of state intervention, whereby management of state-owned hotels, travel agencies, and transportation companies, as well as "scenic spots" in a number of provinces and municipalities, was transferred to municipal tourism corporations. For instance, in Shaanxi, the Qin emperor's terra-cotta army in Xi'an and the sacred mountain Huashan are both controlled by the Shaanxi Tourism Corporation (*Tourism Tribune* 2001:12). These corporations are registered as businesses, but they are managed by former or current officials, and the state and its officials remain by far their largest stakeholders (Qian 2003:157). As the chairman of the board of Beijing's Capital Tourism Group (*Shoudu Lüyou Jituan*) admitted in 2001,

today, tourism development everywhere remains basically a government
activity . . . despite the establishment of a number of tourism groups, a
large number of them has not yet separated government from enterprise;
the government often pushes the development of the industry through
corporate activity. (*Tourism Tribune* 2001:15)

Since tourism corporations do not have exclusive control over a geographic area but are allowed to compete with each other as well as with other developers, they have so far produced an ever-greater proliferation of similar projects instead of differentiated marketing. Tourism corporations, charged with maximizing income rather than with civic boosterism, promote tourism to specific sites, rather than to regions. Tourist information offices do not exist—except those set up by local entrepreneurs for foreign backpackers.

Most tourism development projects are joint ventures between state actors (governments, tourism corporations, or state enterprises) and private investors, in which the state party invests no cash but holds veto power. The two parties can be connected through individuals holding positions in state bodies but acting as private entrepreneurs. Often, the private investor is an ostensibly foreign business, registered abroad or in Hong Kong and thus eligible for tax incentives, but operating with money funneled out of mainland China. Sometimes a government official heads both the domestic and the foreign investing party. For instance, Qiao Yu, quoted above as director of the Badaling Special Zone, is simultaneously general manager of Badaling Tourism Corporation and chairman of the board of Badaling Tourism Development (Hong Kong) Ltd. (Qiao 2001:43). Another example of direct and indirect government involvement is the Nanshan Cultural Tourism Zone, the largest tourism development on Hainan Island, opened in 1998. Although the development has been marketed as an initiative of the newly established—and, of course, government-controlled—Hainan Buddhist Association, it is a joint venture between Sanya Municipal Tourism Development Corporation; Urban (Hainan) Oil and Chemical Industry Ltd.; and Urban (U.S.) Industry Investment Ltd., an affiliate of Urban (Hainan), which in turn is a quasi-state company. The development plan was jointly authored by a consortium of state organizations belonging to the culture bureaucracy, including the China Buddhist Cultural Institute, the China Ethnic Association, and the China History Museum (Li Yiping 2003:439–40). It is the state's involvement in the development of tourist spaces, rather than the inherent commercial logic of that development, that causes the kind of uniform visuality that makes the central squares of Chinese cities, the location and pose of statues, and the content of slogans so predictable. Although the actual repertoire of visual elements has changed greatly in the last twenty years, the symbolic logic of visual centralism has, thanks to the dizzying speed of urban construction, actually become more omnipresent than in its Soviet homeland.

All tour operators and almost all travel agencies in China—except some small ones catering to foreign backpackers—are state-owned, making the travel business one of the least free sectors of the retail economy. Although formally independent market actors, most travel agencies descended in the 1980s and 1990s from branches of three national travel agencies, whose "parent organizations"—following a modified Soviet model—were the National Tourism Administration, the Overseas Chinese Affairs Bureau, the central trade union, and the Communist Youth League. Other travel agencies have been started by state enterprises such as provincial railways or bus transportation companies, ministries, or "mass organizations" such as women's federations. In a kind of clandestine privatization common in Chinese state enterprises, however, individual managers have been allowed to operate as "contractors" (chengbao) of the state travel agencies, conducting their own business in exchange for paying an agreed profit quota to the mother company (Qian 2003:147, 156). Overlaps between businesses and parent organizations and a culture of centralization and hierarchy live on despite fierce competition between the agencies. The intertwining of travel agencies and their supervisory bodies is tellingly illustrated by facts such as the accommodation of the Sichuan Province Tourism Administration in the same building as the Sichuan branch of China Travel Service. Some travel agency catalogues carry prefaces by tourism officials.

No doubt largely due to the embedding of travel agencies in the bureaucratic culture of state enterprises combined with the chengbao system, travel agencies in China are amazingly flexible in some ways but utterly inflexible in others. In the middle of the night, one can buy a travel package over a round-the-clock hotline and be picked up at the desired location the next morning. But most agencies offer exactly the same packages, and should one want something other than a package tour—even simply information—the agencies cannot help. Tourists choose between agencies based on price, reliability, and quality of service—as inferred from a known name or from affiliation with a higher-ranking state organization—rather than based on a difference in itineraries offered or in market segments targeted. In this way, tourism as a market appears to be less differentiated than the market of consumer goods, dominated by private—or, perhaps more precisely, more strongly privatized—enterprise. The rapid growth of the tourism market and the protection of every tourism development from bankruptcy by some state entity have allowed travel agencies to increase business without differentiation.

In addition to wielding effective control as stakeholders in infrastructural development and travel agencies, state actors—a hierarchy of provincial, prefectural, and county tourism bureaus with "guidance" from the National Tourism Authority—approve tour routes (lüyouxian) and "ethnic tourist villages" (Oakes 1998:159). In 1998, the Tourist Encyclopedia of China's Famous Scenic Areas (Zhongguo zhuming fengjing mingsheng lüyou daguan) listed eleven "main tour routes" (China Cultural Relics Research Association et al. 1998:430–32). By 2003, 210 villages had been approved as "demonstration objects of folk life, customs, and culture."[3] In principle, these designations do not mean that no organized tours can be conducted to other places, but given their ownership structure, travel agencies strongly rely on them. Therefore, although little or no state funding comes with the designations, they can have a profound effect on local development. Oakes describes how designation as a "cultural preservation village" in a "minority" area of southeastern Guizhou "sought to fossilize certain aspects of minzu (ethnic) cultural tradition, drawing distinct boundaries around local customs, fixing them in time and space and ensuring that they remain encased as exhibits" (Oakes 1998:179). The designations themselves are the result of competition and negotiation between a multiplicity of agencies with different specializations (tourism, environmental protection, cultural relics, nationalities) and at different levels (from the local to the national) rather than some list drawn up by a central bureau. In Oakes's case, state and semi-state actors who participated in the process of designating the village through both formal and informal means included the prefectural Cultural Relics Department, Nationalities Affairs Commission and Tourism Bureau, the provincial Nationalities Institute, and the Guizhou Overseas Travel Service (which paid a "hosting fee" to the villages visited by its tour groups) (179–82). Most of these organs shaped development simply by officials "inspecting" the village and providing "guidance" rather than issuing formal directives or funding. Nonetheless, recognition as a "good" tourist village had such a strong effect on tourist flows that hundreds of villages went to tourism bureaus every year with petitions accompanied by photos and recordings of songs (222).

In gated "old towns," government intervention is more direct. Zhouzhuang, the "Number One Water Town of China," was a personal project of the town's party secretary: he even wrote the official song that boatwomen sing while paddling tourists in the canals (Becker 2004). At the "old town" of Lijiang in Yunnan—the UNESCO World Heritage Site whose model Songpan's tourism officials hoped to follow—the county government revitalized two street festivals, embarked on a campaign of "civilizing the local residents," and formed a "special unit to reform and popularizes [sic] the traditional dress" of the Naze (Naxi) ethnic group (Lijiang 2001). In addition to protection measures, it demolished "inappropriate buildings," "rebuilt" historical buildings in the "style of the Ming dynasty," and resettled two-thirds of the households formerly resident in the old town. Anyone wishing to move into the old town must apply to the police. The traditional dress unit commissioned the design of new "traditional dress" that met "the young peoples [sic] need," appealed for "more people to dress in the new costumes," and made their wearing compulsory "for people who work in the hospitality sector," regardless of ethnicity (ibid.).[4] In Pingyao, as well as the "water town" of Zhouzhuang, a significant part of the population was removed in the course of tourism development, and both Zhouzhuang and Tongli, another "water town," demolished and "rebuilt" buildings. Tongli, with other "water towns," has formed a committee to apply for World Heritage status (Becker 2004).

Now that tourism has become a major income generator, state officials want as much of it as they can get, and in most cases, their idea of attracting tourists away from competing destinations is to offer more, more "developed" and more "modern" destinations. Conflicts of interest between departments and officials can be over development strategies—local officials usually being more "pro-development" and those at the national level more "pro-conservation"—but much more commonly, they are about who gets a higher share of the profits of development.

Intangible Presence: Cultural Control

While the state rarely intervenes directly in the details of development, it sponsors a discursive regime in which scenic spots and their state-endorsed hierarchy are tools of patriotic education and modernization, and in which the state has the ultimate authority to determine the meaning of the landscape. The sets of views that circulate of China's cities today owe as much to the standard sets of Soviet postcards—which, next to a few churches or old buildings, always showed the same statues of Lenin, modernist "palaces," and views of traffic on broad avenues, thus emphasizing the Soviet over the local—as to pre-modern Chinese view albums.

Borrowing the framework of Ong's (1997) analysis of Chinese transnationalism, Oakes notes the synergy in the new tourist economy between the state wishing to "fix the boundaries of a unique and essential China" and the desire of Chinese capitalists from outside China to invest in "tourist landscapes that symbolize a traditional Chinese cultural core for the new Pacific Century based in flexible accumulation" (Oakes 1998:48). Oakes emphasizes that though this synergy works in the construction of theme parks (and scenic spots), it masks an inherent conflict between a territorial-statist and a cultural interpretation of Chinese modernity (48). These divergent interpretations could manifest themselves in different narratives constructed for tourist sites. But up till now, the space within which investors, UNESCO, local authorities, guidebooks, tour guides, and tourists have been able to invest sites with meaning has been constrained by the discursive regime. At this level, the significance of UNESCO's World Heritage stamp lies not so much in its approving individual spots as in its restoration of China's "five-thousand-year-old superior culture" to its rightful place. Scenic spots, as well as theme parks, with their celebration of China as a harmonious multiethnic community with a glorious history, are a form of "indoctritainment" (Sun 2003:191). As Ann Anagnost has written, citing Benedict Anderson in her analysis of Splendid China, the "quotidian reproducibility" of the state's "regalia" by the desirability of the consumption of iconic sites collected in one place in one's leisure time revealed the "real power of the state" (Anderson 1983:183, quoted in Anagnost 1997:174). Splendid China's endorsement by the state, indeed, came from the highest level: Chairman Jiang Zemin visited it in 1992 and praised its "patriotic message" (Oakes 1998:51).

Encasement and the appearance of mass tourism contradict the values of popular Western ecological discourse. But our fellow tourists at Jiuzhaigou did not see the changes that have taken place since their first visit as contradictory to the language of "sustainable development." Their view was in line with the way the Chinese state often uses environmental discourse: as part of its "civilizing" and modernizing pedagogy. A 1999 book on tourism development, emphasizing sustainable and "green" development, describes the tasks of developing "green scenic spots" as follows:

At all kinds of scenic spots, we must forcefully increase greening and beautification, creating a good environment. Furthermore, we must promote hygiene, safety, civilization, refinement (youya), and engage in recycling, meeting the requirements of sustainable development on all accounts. (Wei et al. 1999:17)

From this angle, teaching people more "advanced" behaviors—for example, not littering, but perhaps also moving them into "more modern" living conditions—and obtaining international endorsement for "sustainable development" are above all aspects of "marching towards the world" (zou xiang shijie), an oft-repeated phrase on billboards and in newspapers. In some situations, this allows the environmental discourse to be used as a cover-up for unpopular measures and even naked abuse of power. This was clearly the case at Kuku Nor, the largest lake in China and a nature reserve, when I visited it in 2003. Kuku Nor on the Tibet-Qinghai Plateau, still in its early phase, was the most extreme example of an encased tourist development that I have experienced.

On the east side of the lake (which can be visited from Xining, the provincial capital of Qinghai, in a day trip), there is only one site that receives tourists. This site, called "151" because it lies at a distance of 151 kilometers from Xining, comprises a few hundred meters of the lakeshore and several hotels and restaurants, hermetically sealed by a fence. It is managed by the quasi-state-owned Qinghai Province Kuku Nor Tourism Development Company. It is labeled a Provincial-Level Patriotic Education Site, and the brass tablet announcing that distinction is displayed next to the entrance to the main hotel. It is presumably intended to designate the lake, but in practice is understood to apply only to the fenced area.

Everyone who wants to see the lake must pay an entrance fee. Local Tibetans who live next to "151" told me that they were not allowed to walk to the lakeshore except through the gate, and if they were caught doing so, they faced a fine. Tibetan herders who live around the lake consider it sacred, but the only stupa (sacred structure) around was located—probably moved to or newly constructed—in the fenced area. For tourists, accessing the lakeshore outside of the controlled area is difficult: they have to walk about one kilometer up to the motorway and then back down through a field between the fence of this site and that of what looks like a holiday village construction site next door. Those Tibetans who do business—sell souvenirs or offer horse rides—inside the area have to pay a share of the income to the site management, yet, at the time of my visit, no one engaged in any of these activities outside the site, suggesting that they were being prevented from doing so. Though the goods and services offered are similar to Songpan, here no contact takes place between visitors and locals outside the site. The nature of the interaction on the site itself, too, is very different from that in Songpan: Tibetans here are mostly children dressed in elaborate ethnic costumes, accompanied by adults who assault tourists with offers to take photos with the children for a fee or to go riding. By contrast, no one offers boat rides. Fishing boats are forbidden. The only way to go out on the lake is to join a group on a large tourist motorboat of a company operating from "151."

The nature reserve administration does not have an office on the site. But next to it, on the motorway, the administration has posted a sign that reads,

"Worshippers and trespassers not allowed because of strong wind and waves in the summer and thin ice in the winter." The ban on fishing boats is also justified by environmental reasons. The China Travel Service guide who accompanied a group I joined for the boat ride told me that fishing boats were not allowed because Kuku Nor is a sacred lake for Tibetans and must be kept clean. Fishing for Kuku Nor's only fish, called *huangyu* in Chinese, is forbidden, as the *huangyu* is a protected species. Nonetheless, all restaurants in the area sell it. However, while those on the site feature it openly on their menus, those outside offer it as a forbidden fruit, their owners claiming to be afraid of fines.

At Kuku Nor, then, environmental discourse is employed in a completely farcical fashion. Not only are locals here deprived of their traditional lifestyle, but also the lakeshore controlled by the site is littered with bottles and rubbish, while outside the fence it is much cleaner.

This instance of "pedagogical abuse" is doubtless the result of corruption in a remote and poor area and should not be attributed broadly to "the state." Nonetheless, what has enabled it is the channeling of tourism development through the organizational and discursive spaces of government bureaucracy. This process affects not only the economics of tourism, but more importantly its cultural grammar, by enforcing a kind of narrative uniformity and ensuring that the affective and sensual experiences of the places as well as their narratives of history and geography conform to the state-endorsed "structure of feeling" (Williams 1961). This mechanism—which functions in much of Chinese public culture, from the development of urban space to filmmaking—further amplifies the homogeneity of tourism development projects, which in any case often are crash copycat developments by entrepreneurs and municipalities desirous of rapid profits from the tourism boom.

Scenic Spots and "Indoctritainment"

Chris Rojek describes the endowment of tourist sites with a set of cultural references as "indexing," which he defines as the creation of "an index of representations; that is, a range of signs, images and symbols which make the site familiar to us in ordinary culture" (1997:53). One result is that when the site—the Sphinx or the Sydney Opera House, for example—is visited, it is compared to this index, and it may be disappointing if "the site is not as breathtaking as one had been led to believe. The sky is not the right color or the building materials look more weathered" (54). Moreover, tourists and tourism developers can consciously or unconsciously create new tourist sites by "dragging" "images, symbols and associations," via "advertising, cinematic use of key sights and travelers tales," into a new index of representation. Rojek illustrates this process by pointing to the construction of Kazimierz as "the Jewish quarter of Krakow" following the 1994 release of the film *Schindler's List*, whose story takes place in that neighborhood, long ago cleansed of any relics of a Jewish past but today studded with klezmer bars and "Jewish" curio shops. Other well-known examples are the development of tourist attractions based on the fictional home of Anne of Green Gables (the heroine of a series of novels by Canadian author Lucy Montgomery) in Prince Edward Island and on the British writer Beatrix Potter and her story of Peter Rabbit in the Lake District, and most recently the boom of *Lord of the Rings* tourism to New Zealand, where figures from the film have even appeared on the planes of the national airline. This process of dragging cultural referents onto a landscape is similar to the endless creation of themed "cultural" sites and routes in China, from the use of the mythical Sani woman Ashima as "both Ms. Nationality Unity (*minzu tuanjie*) and Ms. Local Color (*difang tese*) in the Stone Forest" (Swain 2001:134) to "Miao fortification culture" (Oakes 1998:144) and varieties of "liquor culture" and "tea culture."

Rojek sees indexing and dragging as features of postmodernity enabled by televisual cultures (1997:70–71). He argues that tourist sites rely on distinctions that mark them as extraordinary places, and this demarcation is "reinforced by representational codes and routines of sight-seeing." It is up for debate as to whether there are some supra-cultural universals—e.g., natural features—that mark extraordinariness, but in most cases, the distinction is culturally coded. Televisual culture has undermined the distinction between the ordinary and the extraordinary and made it less fixed, but it has also created new possibilities for creating extraordinariness by indexing and dragging. For Rojek, this is related to the emergence of the "post-tourist" sensibility, whereby the quest for authenticity is less of an attraction than the experience of switching codes or rules of patterned behavior.

Rojek's argument is based on Western success stories of themed landscapes. These fit with his framework of postmodernity in that they use themes that are hard to define in relation to the national. Landscape and travel imagery have played a prominent role in constructing a national culture in nineteenth- and twentieth-century nationalism in the United States (see Löfgren 1999:35) and Europe (see, e.g., Koshar 2000; Edensor 2002; McReynolds 2003), which, at its heyday, was accompanied by the same vision of modernization—and in the United States and Russia, "civilization" of recently colonized peoples—through tourism as is found in China. "Sacred sites" of "national cultures" continue to be important tourist destinations (see Rojek and Urry 1997:12). But in today's Western tourism, such sites are rarely themed because the notion of authenticity is central to most heritage tourism, and even when they are themed (such as "Braveheart Country" as described by Edensor, or St. Augustine or Plymouth Rock in the United States), they represent only one of many possible readings of the landscape, as indexing and dragging practices in the media are multiple and contested. The themed sites featured in Rojek's argument are based on a play with fiction or on ambivalent readings of history (such as *Schindler's List*) and fit well with the "post-tourist" sensibility. The development of Hill Top, the home of Beatrix Potter in the Lake District, an area of Northwestern England whose mainstream index is related to Wordsworth and "English heritage," into a Peter Rabbit site has largely been the result of massive interest from Japanese tourists, and it has encountered resistance from both the National Trust, which owns the house (Rea 2000:640), and local residents. As Edensor points out, "carefully stage-managed spaces may be transformed by the presence of tourists who adhere to different norms" and by the varying nature of performances staged on them, some of which may be improvisatory, non-conformist, ironic, cynical, or resistant (Edensor 2001:64–78). The examples he cites, from India, include cross-dressing by French tourists taking part in a costumed "Village Night," thereby disrupting the script of the performance; English tourists refusing to board the bus when their group was supposed to leave the Taj Mahal and go shopping; and Americans striking mock photo-taking poses in front of the Taj. In addition, it is a common occurrence for Western tourists to refuse to remain within the enshrined site altogether and instead wander off into adjacent areas "where performances without parameters can be entertained" (77).

In China, however, authenticity has not been a concern of the modern, and theming is not necessarily a product of the postmodern. "Culture" and "development" are seen as synergetic rather than antithetical. More often than not, theming is in fact embedded in the high modern project of the Chinese nation-state. Crucially, indexing in Chinese (tele)visuality is part of state-supervised "indoctritainment," and as such, it is not free for contestation by viewers but instead subject to hegemonic rules of content and language—or, to use Wanning Sun's term, "semiotically overdetermined" (Sun 2003:205). There can only be one index of representation for each mingsheng within the seamless flow of visual representations of the nation, from the endless reproductions of Tiananmen Square and sunrise on Mount Tai to China Central Television's Spring Festival Gala that, with its ethnic songs and dances, "five-thousand-year-old traditional culture," and landscape clips, serves as the yearly master recital of national imagery, turned into a modern, global media event (Sun 2002:159–63; see also Gladney 1994). And each file has its place in the filing cabinet of the nation: some characterized by "objectively documented," internationally unique, or superior natural features; some by great persons or events in the canon of Chinese history; and some by the primeval exoticity of the happy ethnic groups that represent the nation's regions. To use another common metaphor, each stage has only one performance: unlike Edensor's cynical, ironic, or resistant tourists, one encounters no dissent at scenic spots. Instead, some Chinese backpackers claim simply to stay away from scenic spots altogether. When Zhang Yimou filmed one of the battle scenes of his celebrated nationalistic film Hero (2002) in Jiuzhaigou, it resulted not in the addition of a film theme to the site (as was the case in Kazimierz, Poland), but in the addition of another layer of meaning to Jiuzhaigou—completely unknown until only recently—as a national landscape.[5] Framed by an internationally endorsed environmental discourse and (now) steeped in national history, Jiuzhaigou thus becomes, perhaps, the modern Chinese landscape, performing a function not unlike that of Yellowstone—an oft-cited model in the sustainable tourism discourse in Southwest China—for the United States at an earlier time.

State, Media, and Market as Co-Producers of the Tourist

Analyzing the representation of monuments in Chinese history textbooks, Nicola Spakowski points out the timeless and "totalizing view of built structures as monuments symbolizing the greatness of the nation," whether by representing the historical unity of the nation, its "resilience" (shengmingli), its "civilizational evolution" (ideally represented by feats surpassing the contemporary West), or the heroism of individual sacrifice (1997:291). Thus, a 1992 textbook entitled Patriotic Stories (Ai zuguo di gushi) says of the Great Wall: "Its history is long, it is lofty and grand; it has few parallels on Earth, and it witnesses the high intelligence and strength of will of the Chinese nation" (Ying 1992:2:22, quoted in Spakowski 1997:301).

FIG.19. *Trilingual (Chinese, English, Japanese) promotional brochure of Wuzhen Tourism Corporation, 2003. Author's collection.*

Something similar can be found in tourism. No site is allowed to escape this totalizing view and mean something ambiguous, purely local, or purely playful. At first sight, the remodeled "old towns," like the "water towns" or Pingyao in Anhui, appear to be akin to German towns on the "Romantic Route," Rothenburg or Dinkelsbühl, standing only for their own past, not for the nation's (fig. 19).

It appears that their "developers" wish to communicate, as did their German colleagues, an extraordinariness that lies in the towns' quaint charm, not in any larger significance. Indeed, the bilingual tourism booklet published by the Tourism Corporation of Zhujiajiao invites visitors to this "water town" near Shanghai with these words:

The beauty of its waters, the antiqueness of its bridges, the mysteriousness of its paths, the seclusiveness of its alleys, and the exquisiteness of its gardens all will attract your admiration when you tread on the stone-paved streets, explore the deep alleys, walk on the arched stone bridges, and sail on the little boat.

But Ann Anagnost suggests, on the other hand, that the function of old towns is to reconstruct "the antiquity of the nation in the very process of its commodification" (1997:166). What these towns contribute to the nation is a visual sense of continuity: a tenet parroted incessantly in the "indoctri-tainment" theme of the "five-thousand-year-old superior culture." Even the creation of Shangri-La County, a development that appears to the Western observer as an example of postmodern playfulness, in fact constitutes a seri-ous competitive claim, as the fictional nature of the Shangri-La story is played down and forgotten. The making of the Chinese tourist, just like the mak-ing of the "new migrant," is a project in which the state, the media, and the market play complementary roles. I therefore do not share Eileen Walsh and Margaret Swain's (2004) characterization of Chinese tourists as "post-tourists." Walsh and Swain join others writing against "tourism-as-homogenization" and observe, similarly to Oakes (1998), that Chinese tourists realize they are being shown staged performances and yet appreci-ate, even expect, them. They conclude that Chinese tourists can be seen both as "more naïve," in that they do not question the authenticity of the sites, and "more sophisticated," in that they "play along" despite being aware of their "staged" nature. This interpretation highlights the liberating poten-tial of Chinese tourism despite its highly regimented nature and reminds us that "whether we define the 'people' as agents or dupes . . . the issue of PLEASURE is critical" (Jing Wang 2001:49). Nonetheless, one should ask how the tourist's pleasure is generated. Writers critical of the "tourism-as-homogenization" view celebrate the diversity of the ways tourist sites are consumed, regardless of the intent of their producers (e.g., Edensor 1998). In China, one sees little of that diversity, and that, I suggest, has to do with how seriously tourists take their "play." When Wei Xiaoan et al. (1999:231) write that ancient relics, "in a sense, could also be understood as theme parks built by people in antiquity," there is no irony here; after all, the authors are happy with the proliferation of theme parks in China, which they see as one area in which the country's tourism has caught up with world trends (Wei et al. 1999:230). Just as tourist enclaves in China are not separated from but play an important role in the national body, just as consumption is not just play but an act of partaking in modernity, the experience of performances and participation in play at these sites is not an ironic postmodern distancing of the self from "reality" by acting out a fantasy;[6] on the contrary, it is partaking in the rehearsal of a high modern hegemonic discourse.

Nowhere is the state's desire to control files of representation clearer than in the publication of tour guides' talks, a genre apparently peculiar to China. Such books as *Superior Guide's Talks* (Youxiu daoyouci), *Ten Great Chinese Tour Guides* (Zhongguo shi jia daoyou), or *The Best of Sichuan Tour Guides' Talks* (Sichuan daoyouci jingxuan) are published, edited, or endorsed by tourism authorities with the aim to promote "correct" representation of tourist sites. The most comprehensive and authoritative of such efforts is the five-volume *Across All China* (Zoubian Zhongguo), published by the National Tourism Administration. The volumes are entitled *Monuments of Patriotic History* (Aiguo shi ji pian), *Folk Customs and Lore* (Minsu fengqing pian), *Landscape and Scenery* (Shanshui fengguang pian), *Cultural Monuments and Relics of Antiquity* (Wen-wu guji pian), and *Overview* (Zonghe pian). Noting that "in recent years, some guides have revealed content that was primitive, superstitious or even contrary to state . . . policy" (*Overview* 2), the editors explain their decision to publish "the best" tour guides' talks on sites ranging from the Forbidden City in Beijing to the Tianchi Lake in Xinjiang in the following way:

> In order to strengthen the construction of spiritual civilization in the tourism industry; to promote China's abundant tourism resources; to promote the achievements of our country's economic construction and tourism industry since Reform and Opening; to foster the patriotic sentiment of all cadres and employees in the tourism profession; to raise the guiding level (*jiangdao shuiping*) of guide personnel; to regulate (*guifan*) guide language . . . we reviewed over 100 . . . tour guides' talks nationwide and selected 31 superior ones. (*Overview* 1)

Although this passage points to tour guides' potential subversiveness, it does not necessarily suggest that many guides radically deviate from canonical interpretations: rather, the editors may be concerned with the proliferation of anecdotes related to contemporary political figures that guides like to weave into their narratives. (For example, on a boat ride at a less-known scenic spot, Golden Lake in Taining County, Fujian, the guide told us that a deer had jumped from one of the rocks we passed into the boat of a former vice governor, and that the official had subsequently been promoted to governor.) In any case, tourism is a realm that the state expects to adhere to the obligation of "correct" language—or in Barbara Mittler's (1997:140) term, "ortholalia"—which attests to its significance in the construction of culture.

Cultural Authority and Resistance

The preceding chapters have shown how the development of commercial tourism in China, controlled by the state and shielded from outside influences by barriers to Chinese citizens' international travel, has (re)created a hegemonic discourse of what constitutes a tourist site and a set of hegemonic representations for the particular sites as they fit into the "nationscape." The degree to which the state has been involved in the production of tourism, in what appears to be an innocuous sphere of the market, is perhaps surprising. Then again, the production of a master narrative on national landscapes by a party-state is perhaps not. A more poignant question is to what extent this project has gone unchallenged. Many states have, after all, produced hegemonic narratives of landscape at various points in history—but perhaps more important is the question of whether tourist practices have actually conformed to those narratives. Much of the recent critique of the earlier writing on "tourism-as-homogenization" has focused on the agency of (Western) tourists, pointing out that though they may be subjected to mass-produced "staged attractions," they consume them in divergent and subversive ways, such as, in the simplest case, ignoring the guide's explanations and wandering off with a beer or an ice cream. MacCannell, for example, cites Urry's *The Tourist Gaze* (1990) to point out that "if we over-emphasize the production side in our research, we may be falsely led to conclude that tourist behavior is uniform and mechanistic" (MacCannell 2001:24). Indeed, even a writer openly nostalgic for the Soviet ideals of tourism dismisses the All-Union Tourist Trek to Places of Battle Glory as a series of "ideological acts [with] no place for actual tourist treks" attended mainly by Komsomol (Communist Youth League) functionaries (Usyskin 2000:195). And yet, especially if the late "socialist" Chinese state does not speak with a single voice on tourism or anything else—as I have argued above—why is it that the voices one ends up hearing are nonetheless so similar?

None of the travel agents, other tourism professionals, and locals involved in the tourism industry that we spoke to, even those in Songpan who catered to Western backpackers, challenged the concept of the scenic spot. Whether this model of tourism is more or less beneficial to the economic and cultural "empowerment" of local residents than more low-impact, individual tourism is open to question. It has been shown at several scenic spots (e.g., Duang 2000) that most of the entrepreneurs who profit from large-scale tourism at scenic spots are not locals, but rather outsiders who move in with tourism and are not necessarily interested in conservation. We observed the same in Jiuzhaigou. Yet although locals in Chuanzhusi performed only peripheral jobs, most were happy about "development." Even while professing a "hatred" of "Chinese rule," a Tibetan tour guide in Yunnan, interviewed by Litzinger (2004), made clear his preference for organized tourism to low-scale mountaineering, since independent groups of mountaineers were more likely to circumvent his services. It has also been suggested that corralling tourists into "staged attractions" makes their impact more manageable for locals, thus giving the latter more say in how much "disruption" they wish to accommodate (Buck 1977).

What I am interested in, however, is the resistance of the tourists themselves to the hegemony of the scenic spots. As we have seen, fellow travelers in our tour group, as well as other group tourists we have spoken to, may have been skeptical of the "quality" of sites they were shown or of the truthfulness of superlative and historical claims made about them, and they may have complained about the quality of the service; but they did not question or deviate from the basic pattern of sightseeing. Yet several times, asking tourists whether they had considered traveling alone, we received replies that reflected awareness of the Western hierarchy of "traveler" over "tourist." A young English graduate from Guangzhou in our group told us: "I know that foreigners like to travel alone, with a backpack and so on. And we as young people would like that too." For tour guide Xiao Ma, too, the attraction of individual travel seemed to lie in its association with the West: "Actually, it is you foreign friends who know what travel really is: take a backpack and go riding. I (too) think it is better to go alone." A middle-aged cadre from Kashgar responded: "When I have time I travel alone, taking buses. That way I can decide how long to spend where. That's the best. But when I am pressed for time I travel with a group."

A small but increasing number of mostly young Chinese do choose to travel on their own. In China, this is called "self-service travel" (zizhuyou) to distinguish it from ordinary, group travel. Groups of "jeep safari" enthusiasts with names like Cross-Wilderness Federation (*Yueye Lianmeng*) and Wilderness Warriors (*Yezhanpai*) have sprung up across China's large cities. Places like Shidu near Beijing offer horse riding and bungee jumping. Walsh and Swain (2004) write about young Chinese who drive jeeps to Lugu Lake in Yunnan, stay and eat with local families, and go hiking around the lake. Guo Shang of Shunjiang Horse Treks told us that most Chinese coming to ride horses in Songpan found out about it through Chinese backpacker Web sites.

In the 2000s, books targeting this group emerged, and by our visit in 2003, they were prominently displayed at bookshops in Chengdu and Lanzhou, with many teenagers and young people browsing through them. However, it is important that—unlike the mainstream tourism discourse, generated in a top-down fashion by the state and state-affiliated large tourism developers—the backpacker discourse first emerged on the Internet, in bulletin-board discussions that foster competing information.

While these tourists, too, pursue the internal exotic—most of the online accounts and all but one of the backpacker books I have seen are about the mountainous and desert regions of Western China's ethnic periphery: Xinjiang, Tibet, Qinghai, and Gansu—they engage in an alternative discourse of travel, self-consciously embracing the Western model of the tourist as solitary adventurer and sometimes openly declaring individual tourism as a mark of modernity. What they are after is the "simplicity," "closeness to nature," "spirituality," or "sincerity" they find in those remote locations. They express these pursuits in highly charged language with a strong New Age flavor. As one backpacker wrote in an article entitled "I really hope to be reborn as a bird," "What I like most of all is that feeling of freedom and independence" (Lin 2002b). The backpacker Web site http://www.fidotour .com (accessed September 20, 2003) has the following message in English on its opening page:

> FIDO is for FIDO, FIDO against no one.
> FIDO is youth, FIDO has no age.
> FIDO sees everything, FIDO judges nothing.
> FIDO is innocent, FIDO is powerful.
> FIDO comes from the past, FIDO is the future.

Others who cater to backpackers also emphasize the spiritual fulfillment they derive from this new experience. The Suoma Hotel was opened by a young man in Chengdu after returning from a backpacking trip to Germany: he wanted to have a "European-style youth hostel" to cater to backpackers, yet because of the SARS scare, most of the guests in the first year were Chinese. The manager of the hotel had previously worked as a cook at a youth hostel in Xi'an and said, "From the beginning, I liked backpackers. There was this couple with children, there were the French people who traveled on bicycles, there was the writer, the PhD in Chinese. . . . I felt happy with them." Several of the tourists to Lugu Lake in Walsh and Swain's study stayed there for weeks, "contemplating the lake," writing poetry, or reading "classical philosophy."

Seeking authenticity in the Chinese landscape and minorities, this tourist counterculture eschews scenic spots, performances, hotel lobbies with four clocks over the reception desk, and seemingly everything else that goes with mainstream tourism in China. For example, the author of an attractively designed book carrying the English title *A Cowhide Book of Tibetan Lands: The Feeling of Pick up Your Backpack and Go!*, using the pen-name "Straight," explicitly excludes "scenic spots" from his book (Yizhi 2002). Instead, the tourist counterculture embraces frugality, individualism, and seclusion, to some extent alluding to the classical trope of the Buddhist/Taoist recluse. A contributor who recommended horse riding in Songpan on the website of Green Wilderness Self-Service Outdoors Activities (Lüye zizhu waihu huodong), a group in Beijing (http://www.lvye.org, accessed September 20, 2003), wrote that this was "not our usual idea of a tour guide waving a little flag calling out to tourists to move on: they (the guides) are all pure and simple local folk." A January 25, 2003 posting by a Chengdu travel agency on Sichuan Tourism Forum (Sichuan Lüyou Luntan, http://www.travelbbs.com/songpan/about .htm) advertising horse riding in Songpan said, "Unlike the normal tour group . . . we will certainly not make you shop etc." and warned, "Those without a community spirit need not apply."

Despite the effort of the backpacker discourse to differentiate backpackers from mainstream tourists, it shares certain features with the language of the latter. Although it valorizes authentic experiences, it is not concerned with the "authenticity" of art or architecture in the same way Western tourist discourse is. Most of the Web sites and books are strongly focused on the experiences and feelings of one particular author and on his personal itinerary. Unlike *Lonely Planet*, the *Rough Guide*, or Western backpackers' Web sites, they do not attempt to cover all possible destinations and aim primarily to describe feelings rather than to convey practical information. The *Cowhide Book* and its analogues provide little historical or political context or opinion on whether or not a place is worth going to, all crucial features of English-language backpacker guidebooks. Backpackers' Web sites in English are focused on exchanging information and have popular bulletin boards; by contrast, none of the Chinese ones had any real discussion. Western backpackers' guidebooks and Web sites can make new destinations fashionable; Chinese guidebooks lack the intention and the power to do so.

Whereas Western backpacker discourse distinguishes itself from the mainstream tourist discourse by being down-to-earth and even cynical about tourist activities, the Chinese backpacker language is highly poetic, focused on experiencing the sublime, with no room for reflection on tourism or irony. For instance, the *Cowhide Book*'s section about Langmusi (Dagtsanglhamo), a popular Chinese backpacker destination on the Sichuan-Gansu border, relates the tale of the town's name—derived from a Tibetan monastery— and suggests an idyllic atmosphere. It does not mention that the monastery in its current form was built in 1980, or that the town is the site of very extensive construction work (Yizhi 2002:416). Similarly, most of the place descriptions in *Traversing China on Foot* (Zhongguo tubu chuanyue; English title: *A Guide for Chinese Hikers*) consist of folk legends and rituals but do not mention whether or not the place is worth stopping at (Shaanxi 2003). Even though sites of mass tourism, with their development and crowds, seem to stand for everything the authors of these books want to avoid, they—and more surprisingly, participants of online backpacker discussions—do not criticize or satirize these sites and their practices the way their Western counterparts do.[7] Most authors ignore them, even when a route they are describing passes right through one. Thus, writers on both the Lüye Web site and the Self-Service Travel Network site (Zizhu lüyou wang, http://www.17lai.com) described Jiuzhaigou using the standard brochure terms such as "fairytale world" (tonghua shijie), without reflecting on tourism development there.[8]

The backpacker discourse describes backpacking as a quintessentially modern lifestyle, and as such, it derives its legitimacy from the imagery of Western modernity, together with North Face fleece jackets and Timberland boots and backpacks (fig. 20). In her account of a trip to India in the popular Shanghai-based *Travel Times*, a Chinese female backpacker's joy over the sense of fraternity she experienced with backpackers of other nations leads her to claim that "the backpacker tribe is best able to embody a nation's economic strength and its national quality. The fact that Japanese backpackers are found in every corner of the earth is inseparable from Japan's enormous economic strength" (Lin 2002a). She adds: "When American and Japanese

FIG. 20. *The outdoors as new urban lifestyle. Cover of* Travel Times *(Shanghai), July 11–17, 2002. Author's collection.*

backpackers understood that I was traveling alone and stared at me in admiration—I would not have exchanged that feeling of national pride for anything" (Lin 2002b). The triumphalism of this woman's narrative derives from her sense of liberation upon experiencing travel abroad on equal terms with Westerners and Japanese, while most carriers of PRC passports continue to endure humiliation at the hands of immigration officers worldwide. Nonetheless, it is remarkable how much the language of this article echoes the hegemonic, official discourse of Chinese nationalism and modernity that pervades mass tourism.

It would be tempting to see Chinese tourism today as simply an early stage of evolutionary development that the West has also gone through, and most Chinese authors do precisely that (e.g., Wei et al. 1999:93). There is little question that they are correct in expecting that Chinese tourism will become more individual and differentiated with time, just as the share of group tourism has declined in the West since the first charter flight landed in Corsica in 1949 (Löfgren 1999:159). But its share is still high, and in some cases—notably in beach resort tourism—it does produce a uniformity of sites not unlike that in China. "Village fiestas" very similar to China's Ethnic Culture Nights are still regularly presented to European package tourists at peri-Mediterranean beach resorts, so uniform that the only major difference may be in the "welcome drink": ouzo for Greece, mint tea for Morocco. The developers of resorts in Turkey, Egypt, the Canary Islands, Majorca, or Crete copy each other. Sand, palm trees, white plastic chairs, and a kind of beach English are imported, and tour guides and "animation teams" circulate between the localities, resulting in an "amazing continuity in the structure of package tours to the Mediterranean, among localities and tour companies alike" (185–94).

But even if we were to back away from the distinction I have made between "national" sites—which must, in the West, be "authentic"—and the extra-territorial, playful nature of beach resorts and theme parks, we could not ignore the fact that, as Löfgren documents, the appearance of the charter tourist on Mediterranean beaches was accompanied with a barrage of protest against the "five S" (sun, sea, sand, sex, and spirits), not so much by highbrow intellectuals as by writers of letters to the popular press. Evelyn Waugh's maxim that "the tourist is the other fellow" is not class-specific: travel agents, as in Thomas Cook's times, market even the most mass-oriented of their products as distinctive and authentic, and package tourists complain about overcrowding and inauthenticity. If anything, these comparisons point toward a more general point differentiating the cultural history of modernity in China from that in the West: the absence of a civilisatory dictatorship of the highbrow over the lowbrow, a strict normative hierarchy of "high culture" over "popular culture." In Europe—including, in some form, the Soviet Union—the grip of the highbrow fastened with modernization; but in post-imperial and especially post-Cultural Revolution China, it loosened. The contents of brochures produced by Chinese tourism authorities—like Jiang Zemin's praise of the film Titanic—cannot be attributed simply to the "low quality" of the official in charge; they reflect the fact that the highbrow has little to no role as a standard in public discourses of "cultural correctness."

A comparison between the recent development of mass tourism in China and in Russia reinforces the point that a unilinear evolutionary scheme is insufficient to explain the Chinese situation. Package tourism in Russia today remains the prevalent form of foreign tourism across a broader range of social classes than in the West. It is not generally seen as culturally inferior, and though its share is already declining, mailing lists with titles like "Learning to Travel on Our Own" (from the Web site http://www.etur.ru) suggest that this process is not an unproblematic one. But domestic tourism in Russia—as evidenced by interviews with tour operators at the 2002, 2003, and 2004 Berlin International Tourism Fairs (ITB)—is overwhelmingly individual and focused on beaches, wellness, wilderness tourism, and *ekstrim*. There are a number of tourism developments, especially in northern Russia, that are themed on the supposed rural essence of "Russian culture," such as a tourist itinerary developed by the Northwestern Administrative District which includes "a Russian wedding" and "fishing Russian style."[9] Mandrogi, a "traditional Russian village," has been built along the popular river route between the Lakes Ladoga and Onega, and all tourist ships stop there. But other regional governments are promoting "active rest in the deep countryside,"[10] such as hiking, rafting, horse riding, and fishing. Karjala in northwestern Russia, Lake Baikal, and the Ural and Altai mountains in Siberia are marketed as ecotourism destinations (see, e.g., Baikaltur 2004). Overall, the sites are fairly diverse, with no unifying narrative, little encasement, and little evidence of the national or the state. Although Russia has nineteen World Heritage sites, the label is hardly ever used in the domestic marketing of nature sites to tourism. While officials at the World Heritage Center believe that "an increase in tourism is an inevitable result of inscription,"[11] this does not seem to have been the case at Russian World Natural Heritage sites, which are not visually identified as such, and even travel agents who offer trips to the areas are not sure where exactly the sites included in the Heritage listings are.

Another relevant comparison is with Japan, a country that shared China's pre-modern ideals of gentry travel along with its canon of *meisho* (Japanese for *mingsheng*) and view albums (Ivy 1995:47), best known in the West from the artist Hiroshige's series of views on the stations of the Tokaido. Japan is the only non-Western country whose tourism practices have been widely acknowledged—and caricatured—and have attracted some research. A number of studies suggest that a state-supervised reinvigoration and nationalization of the *meisho* canon took place as part of the industrialization and modernization efforts of the Meiji reign period (1868–1912; see, e.g., Ivy 1995:32–33). This drive appears to have been not unlike the Chinese state's in the 1980s, but it took place in a global context of high industrial modernity, of which Japan was striving to become a part. Up until the 1960s,

Japanese considered travel as sightseeing—the viewing, often seasonal, of culturally acclaimed landscapes and sites: the cherry blossoms of Yoshino, the autumn leaves of Lake Towada, snow-clad Mount Fuji. Travel to these landscapes was an exercise in confirmation: the sightseer . . . expected no unusual encounters, no solitary experience (keiken). The express purpose of travel was to see what one was supposed to see, to view an already culturally valued scene, and to acquiesce to general opinion. (Ivy 1995:44–45)

Japanese tourists began going abroad in large numbers in the late 1960s. According to Brian Moeran, the first decade of tourism was characterized by an orientation towards sights, with each city being known for a few specific spots—not necessarily those promoted among Western tourists—with well-defined cultural associations (e.g., Lausanne being known for the seat of the International Olympic Committee, Geneva for the room in the University that Rousseau used to sit in, the Rhine for poetry by Heine and Byron, and the Piazza di Spagna for an Audrey Hepburn film scene) (Moeran 1983). By the 1980s, group tourism began to be seen as inferior to individual travel (ibid.), suggesting that some aspects of tourism discourse in Japan were beginning to evolve along a trajectory shared with the West. At the same time, as noted above, Japanese tourists and tourism promoters continued creating new files of representation for sites abroad ("dragging"), as evidenced by the Beatrix Potter and Lucy Montgomery estates, both developed substantially to satisfy the interest of Japanese tourists.

What is interesting here is not whether or not Japanese tourism has, in general, become increasingly similar to Western tourism, but rather the specific factors that have affected its change. The 1970 *Discover Japan* marketing campaign, "the most successful advertising campaign of Japanese history" (Ivy 1995:34), which played a decisive role in the 1970s boom of mass tourism, promoted a discourse that *opposed* the idea of scenic spots. Although the campaign served economic aims—specifically, to increase passenger volume on the national railways—it also fit broadly into the government's aim of promoting a communitarian sense of the nation after what was perceived as the alienating impact of rapid modernization. (A parallel campaign, initiated by the governing Liberal Democratic Party, promoted the idea of the *furusato*, or home village; see Rea 2000:642.) But the chosen strategy was to make Japanese subjects connect to the perceived essence of Japan *individually*. The campaign

advocated a solitary, small-scale form of travel, in which landscapes became settings for miniature dramas of national-cultural and subjective discovery. The landscapes and places depicted and promoted were not the famous icons of Japanese natural beauty and civilization, but obscure, often unnamed scenes. (Ivy 1995:35)

While the campaign's English title and selling lines such as *jisukaba maiserufu* ("discover myself") conveyed the idea of modernity, its insistence on the "natively local" stood, according to Marilyn Ivy, in opposition to the "rationalism and materialism" that was identified as American and, in this view, associated with scenic spots (Ivy 1995:42). The campaign's authors aimed to promote "the discovery of the self that money cannot buy. . . . Therefore, if beautiful scenic photographs function merely to entice people to travel, we must negate that function itself" (43).

A final comparison can be made with Machu Picchu, a World Heritage site (listed in 1983) in a poor region of Peru. The Machu Picchu site has developed in a way that is very different from Jiuzhaigou, and that is largely because of local resistance. As Alexandra Arellano (2004) writes, development of the site for tourism began in earnest in the 1990s, with plans to build a cable car that would have increased the number of visitors from five hundred to four thousand per day. But a coalition of activists, including many from the local tourism sector, successfully campaigned to defeat the project. The dean of the Faculty of Tourism at the University of Cuzco described the project as "go[ing] against the very essence of the beauty of Machu Picchu which is an expression of the ancient science, knowledge and technology" (Arellano 2004). The activists were backed by forceful UNESCO pressure, which criticized harshly "stakeholders . . . act[ing] in their own self-interest" and called for the establishment of an "independent and international" institution to supervise the development of the site (World Heritage Committee 2002). Instead of taking a cable car, an increasing number of tourists now choose a four-day mountain trek that "has become a tourist rite of passage that testifies [to] the 'real Inca experience.' . . . [T]o take a picture of oneself in front of the temple . . . is no longer enough:" the trek is seen as authenticating the experience by—in the words of a foreign tourist—"enter[ing] the city the way the original inhabitants did" (Arellano 2004). Although tourism here is mostly foreign—and Arellano's work does not ask to what extent these norms correspond to locals' preferences—the point is that the coalition of state sponsorship and foreign capital could not follow the Jiuzhaigou path because their views of desirable tourism development were effectively countered by the views of Western ecologists, which were sufficiently widely shared in Peru. In a situation where opinions on the ground were divided, UNESCO sided with the "ecologists."[12] As a result, what was framed as the common interest of humankind prevailed over the national aspect of the site. Thus, "world heritagization," though offering the promise of authenticating sites as "global places" (ibid.) and employing the same ecological discourse on the surface, has produced very different results. (The cable car at Mt. Emei, also a World Heritage site, had at first aroused UNESCO's concern, but eventually, a mission from the World Heritage Center [2001] concluded that it did not have "any significant adverse impact." Unlike the situation at Machu Picchu, UNESCO did not release a detailed report.)

My point here is that, just as there is no single form of modernity, there can be multiple forms of mass tourism. Accounts of tourism provide clues for seeing China, Japan, Russia, and Western Europe as being neither on different points of an evolutionary trajectory of modernity nor on incompatible cultural scales of it, but rather going through a series of staggered configurations, each of which arises through a confluence of related and unrelated, historical and contemporary, material and discursive conditions.[13] Modernity as industrialization and as postindustrial consumption, the building of the national state, and political control have all affected the development of tourism in the West, China, and Japan. The effects they produced may have been rather similar in themselves, but because they stood in different temporal configurations to each other, they ultimately produced different results.

The path taken by the development of Chinese mass tourism is not well explained by generic cultural or historic assumptions of "conformity" attached either to tourism or to China. Meaningful parallels can, for instance, be drawn between the standardization of scenic spots in today's China and the standardization of temple worship and funeral rites in imperial China, a process in which, according to James Watson (1985, 1992), state officials and government-issued manuals were intimately involved. Watson represents the influential view that early in imperial times, illiterate speakers of mutually unintelligible languages were able to identify with a unified China through the state-sponsored practice of shared rituals—or more broadly, rules of propriety (li)—which he calls "orthopraxy." It is tempting to see tourism as one of not so many shared rituals of the reform era, rituals to replace the more coercive yet in some ways similar ones—"loyalty dances," struggle meetings, and annual river dips—of the late Mao years. Yet such historical parallels, in themselves, do no more to *explain* what is happening today than parallels with mass tourism elsewhere. For today's particular practices to emerge in the People's Republic of China, recent developments were necessary that were in no way historically or culturally determined or predictable: the choice of the Mao-era leadership not to employ tourism as a tool of mobilization, the relationship between nationalism and consumption that has developed in post-1978 China, and the ideological erasure of the Mao era by the post-1978 leadership.

"Post-tourism" and the desire for authenticity can be seen as an expression of what Daniel Miller (1994) has called the contradiction between the "transient" and the "transcendent" and identified as a defining feature of modernity. Both Western and Chinese tourism are a pursuit of both the transient and the transcendent, but the nature of these—the relationships between them and the rules governing their pursuit—are differently framed. The question underlying this book, then, has been how the particular framework of cultural authority and the enabling hardware that governs tourism in China today have been created.

Taking my cue from Jing Wang's recommendation to study the Chinese state "in action" (Jing Wang 2001:45), I suggest that the Chinese construction of the tourist site may be useful for understanding the mechanisms by which the Chinese state has so successfully maintained its authority to represent and interpret Chinese culture, and why these representations remain so overwhelmingly uniform despite capitalist competition and what appears to be an increasingly open information and discussion space available to citizens. As Laura Nader has written, "When the use of *social* control becomes less culturally acceptable, especially for the middle class, the use of *cultural* control becomes more central for the mechanics of power" (Nader 1997: 720). *Mutatis mutandis*, this critique, written with Western liberal democracies in mind, appears to fit today's China, where—to paraphrase Lenin— the state is no longer able to apply the forms of social control it did up until the 1980s, and the people no longer want to subject themselves to it. Nader noted that the forces—or perhaps more precisely, the tools—of cultural control "are often non-ideological or anti-ideological, although they are defended in terms of ideological constructs" (ibid.).

In China, cultural control has arguably increased, not decreased, with capitalist competition and increasing flows of information. Others have made that point in studies of high cultural discourse. Of particular note is Geremie Barmé's sophisticated study (1999) of what he calls "the graying of Chinese culture" after 1989, a study in which he draws on Haraszti Miklós's description of 1980s Hungary as "the velvet prison." What these studies underline is the absence of serious challenges to or even reflection on the unitary discourse of culture, even as the state becomes increasingly difficult to pinpoint as the producer of that discourse. While in many other realms linguistic practices diversify, when it comes to "culture" the "ortholalia" characteristic of the more repressive forms of state socialism hold sway. This is one of the more perplexing phenomena in China today and one which political factors are insufficient to explain. References to the absence of an independent intellectual tradition are ultimately tautological, while cultural explanations—even the more sophisticated ones having to do with the history of linguistic practices in written Chinese—get sometimes perilously close to age-old orientalist images of China. The radical claim that "spectacular power may be wielded at a local level by state or official authority, but it is fundamentally however [sic] the same capitalist spectacular power that deprives and suppresses the powerless around the globe" (Lee 2003:61) attempts to solve the problem by sublimating it into a universal, but by doing so it ignores its very core: that power works very differently in different places. The answer must lie, as Barmé suggests, somewhere in the fine structure of the state-economy-culture triangle that defines the current historical moment of the People's Republic of China. But how to put our fingers on it?

The most serious attempts to tackle this question have come from two directions. A number of literary and film scholars have approached it through the production of the cultural imagery of the nation in the realm of cultural politics, semiotics, literature, film, and television.[14] Another approach, taken mostly by anthropologists and sociologists, has been to look at the effects of the emerging culture of urban consumption on subjectivity (e.g., Davis 1999; Chen et al. 2001; Farrer 2002; and Farquhar 2002). Tourism is an arena in which the production of cultural discourse penetrates everyday consumption, one in which Chinese subjects self-consciously consume complex representations of culture and respond to them in quotidian activities.[15] As such, it is a key sphere in which the reinvention of the Chinese subject takes place, and consequently an important area for the state to control. On the other hand, it is a sphere in which, in most cases, the stakes seem low, and control is not exercised by diktat. There is no apparent reason why alternative representations of scenic spots should be censured, unless the spots are part of nationalist or Communist hagiography. Yet the apparently unproblematic internalization of the sites' hegemonic narratives, the absence of even politically innocent challenges to the commodified presence of state symbols at the sites I have visited, and the pervasive sense of the national are striking. The absence of challenges seems not to be because their motive or content would necessarily be seen as subversive, but because the structure of feeling which—(re)produced in semi-structured, semi-spontaneous, semi-coerced, and semi-voluntary acts of the state-market matrix—dominates these landscapes and defines the way tourists negotiate their meanings simply does not allow the production of dissent. More generally (and resonating with the current debate on the "private sphere" in state socialism and in China) tourism demonstrates strikingly the complex ways in which the Chinese state remains imbricated in shaping the everyday practices, lifestyles, and even fashions its citizens pursue.

The short history of commercialized tourism in the People's Republic of China has displayed a view of culture unaffected by the turbulences of the intellectual debates of the 1980s and 1990s. It shows how two complementary discourses—that of a Chinese cultural essence and that equating culture to leisure to consumption to modernity, both generated by state actors in the 1980s and 1990s and legitimized by references to historical continuity—established themselves as a canon of everyday feeling relayed by a booming business serving as an accomplice to "the pedagogical practices of the postsocialist state" (Jing Wang 2001:36–38). Even though the tourism business is, generally, market-driven, consumer-oriented, and by nature global, the presence of the state informs the transmissions between the cultural and the economic that have shaped the directions of tourism's development.

4

SCENIC SPOTS BEYOND THE BORDER

Migration, Tourism, and Cultural Authority

S ince the People's Republic embarked on the modernization drive that
became supreme state ideology and social mantra after 1978, Chinese
citizens have continuously been challenged to travel in multiple ways
(see Rofel 1992). As Xin Liu (1997) has pointed out, a "spatial hierarchy" arose
in which one's "success" as a modern—or "advanced" (xianjin), "civilized"
(wenming), "cultured" (you wenhua), or "high-quality" (you suzhi)—Chinese
subject was linked to mobility. At the pinnacle of that hierarchy was international migration to the United States, the country that most symbolized
global modernity. Migration, having only recently been seen as treachery, was
now reevaluated as an act of patriotic potential: "successful" migrants could
contribute not only to their own modernization and glory but also to that of
the Fatherland (Nyíri 2001). Migrants are symbolic figures because they represent the vanguard of modernity, not only by virtue of their connection to
more "advanced" nations, but also by the very fact of their mobility.

As with its policy reversal on domestic tourism, China changed from a
state that prevented foreign travel to one that encouraged it but attempted
to control its meaning. The public discourse in 1990s China, from academia
to the media, equated travel abroad with migration in pursuit of individual
"development" (fazhan) through education or work and, ultimately and opti-
mally, entrepreneurship. Indeed, the master narrative of the "new migrant"
was one of what Harvey (1989) termed "flexible accumulation." The "new

migrant" was a figure that represented a new, globally modern and yet authentically national—even racial—way of being Chinese. The image was of someone who is successful in the global capitalist economy and rises to a position of economic and even political power in the country that epitomizes modernity and power, the United States, and is able to do so precisely because of certain innate Chinese moral qualities. These include a natural, selfless loyalty to the homeland that manifests itself in donations and investments (Nyíri 2002b). To cite a typical example, a recent paper by a Chinese scholar claimed that new migrants, whose achievements "reflect the national policy of reform and opening and display the Chinese people's talents to the world," have a special "feeling of Chineseness," and "realize that their roots are in Chinese culture" (Ju 2004)

Outside China, this image of the Chinese migrant was met with neo-Yellow Peril images of Chinese migration that circulated in mainstream media in Europe and Asia (and, in part, in America) and frequently associated new migration from mainland China with illegality, crime, and threats to economic security, demographic balance, and public health (e.g., Friman 2002; Lomanov 2002). Nonetheless, the "new migrant" image had a powerful impact on the fashioning of Chinese migrant subjects, on the way migrants saw themselves, their various environments, and their relationship to China and the countries they resided in, and in the way they justified their choices and actions (Nyíri 2002a, 2002b). This was because "new migrant" imagery, carried into individual homes by a burgeoning global Chinese media, gradually replaced locally constructed media discourses (Nyíri 2005). Media adopting this discourse included the satellite channel of China Central Television and private channels with business interests in mainland China and Hong Kong, as well as newspapers published by Hong Kong-based concerns and by new migrants (see Yang 1997; Xudong Zhang 2001a; Nyíri 2002b; and Parker 2003).[1]

World Cities, the "New Migrant," and Chinese Modernity

Overseas Chinese have played central roles in Chinese discourses of a national culture on several occasions in the country's modern history (see, e.g., Duara 1997). Today again, the economic success of overseas Chinese and, in particular, "new migrants," plays a central role in assertions of cultural nationalism. As Rojek and Urry point out, tourism's contribution to the creation of a "national culture" may involve sites across national borders, and this is necessarily the case for diasporic (or transnational) populations (1997:12). For China today, global cities of the West increasingly acquire the meaning of such national sites beyond the border, signifying migrant success through a plethora of films, television dramas, and fiction. Beginning with the hugely successful soap opera based on the 1991 novel *A Beijing Man in New York*, migrants in these accounts play the role of both scout and voyeur for the nation, providing a continuous peep show accompanied by a commentary on foreign localities as backdrops for evolving ways of Chinese life (Sun 2002:67–111). In these books, films, and television programs, Tokyo, Moscow, Paris, and New York are above all sites of an unfolding global Chinese modernity. This function, as Wanning Sun observes, shapes the visual presentation of the cities through

fetishistic uses of clichéd icons of speed, such as cars gliding noiselessly (and seemingly pollution-free) along the surface of highways; power-imposing bottom-up shots of city skylines; and energy, suggested by sweeping shots of multilevel highways. (Sun 2002:77)

Media reports and soap operas about and by "new migrants," along with highly popular foreign (mainly American) television serials, are influential in shaping travelers' expectations of sites outside China, particularly since live reports with "ordinary Westerners" or Western-made documentaries are rarely broadcast. Indeed, Sun observes that Chinese arriving in Australia look for signs of modernity familiar from films, and their absence "can sometimes be as disappointing to Chinese arrivals in the 'New World' as the experience of some Western tourists who arrive in a 'Third World' place and fail to see signs of tradition—that is, 'authenticity'" (Sun 2002:77).

Most commonly, it is Europe, a less familiar migration destination, that is referred to as a "new world" (xin tiandi) in "new migrant" literature. Migrants arriving in Europe, too, look for the signs they have encountered in these soap operas and reports, but these signs are different from those described by Sun. In *Into Europe* (Zouru Ouzhou), a 1999 soap opera produced by Southeast Fujian Television (based on A Hang's novel and directed by Chen Kemin), the episodes open with glamorous shots of Paris, Rome, or Budapest at night, but the daytime scenes portray a continent that is slow, romantic, and lacking in modernity. That modernity is delivered without fail by the new Chinese migrant, the main hero of the series. He arrives in Paris penniless, but within a year, he reveals to a stunned and applauding Parisian audience his plan for an ambitious new construction project. "Ladies and gentlemen!" he announces, pointing to the scheme of a building complex with pagoda-style roofs, "What will be different on the new map of Paris two years from now? The beautiful banks of the Seine will be full of Oriental splendor: the Chinatown Investment and Trade Center!" (Nyíri 2002b). The significance of the "new Chinese" showing Paris—the symbolic center of Europe—the road to modernity is obvious to any Chinese viewer brought up on narratives of how imperialist Europe has both humiliated China and forced it to modernize. The Chinese state looms large in the narrative of the film, which is produced and aired by state broadcasters: the Chinese embassy provides support for the protagonist's project, while funding for it is secured from China.

In series set in Eastern Europe, such as the tellingly named *Yellow Sun on the Danube's Banks* (Duonao hepan di huang taiyang) or *Goodbye, Moscow!* (Bie le, Mosike!), there is less romance and more emphasis on "backwardness" (Nyíri 2002b). But in all of these series, Europe emerges as a network of Chinatowns, Chinese restaurants, and markets selling Chinese goods. "Foreigners" (or "whities," *laowai*)—police, tax officers, entrepreneurs, girlfriends, waiters, secretaries—and their casinos, parks, shopping malls, and swimming pools are not at the nodes of this map but fall in between them, like ethnic "minority" dancers. In fact, the novel *Holy River* (Sheng he) has Hungarian waiters clad in ethnic costume perform a dance for their Chinese boss (Nyíri 2002b).

This view of Europe has been echoed by many migrants I have interviewed in the course of my work in the 1990s and early 2000s. "What's good about Europe is that it's quiet and there are few people. For the rest of it, Shanghai is better. It's more developed," said Sun, a twenty-eight-year-old from Shanghai who worked as a waitress in Budapest. "Italy doesn't have any nice places," agreed her twenty-year-old colleague, Yang, in Prato, Tuscany. Although they had not traveled extensively, their views of Europe were quite set: both ranked Paris as the best place. "A bit more modern, almost like Shanghai," conceded Sun. "The most beautiful city. It's hygienic, and people are civilized," suggested Yang. When asked what specifically there was to see in Paris, Wang, a twenty-year-old who has lived in the Netherlands, Portugal, and Hungary, named "the iron tower and Disneyland." Asked about Eastern European countries, He, a fifty-year-old trader in Budapest, noted that Budapest had the largest underground, while Sofia, Warsaw, and Belgrade did not have one at all (suggesting that they were "less developed"). Similarly, Luo, a factory worker in Treviso, Italy, was impressed with two things about Moscow: the underground and Red Square, with Lenin's mausoleum. These responses clearly reflected the same civilizatory discourse of modernization that we have witnessed at scenic spots.

Other migrants, generally those with more education and those who had spent a longer time in Europe, were more likely to appreciate the "historic" or "romantic" side of Europe despite its "lack of development." "In Europe, if something is beautiful, everyone protects it," noted Zhao, a businesswoman in Budapest; "Historical things are preserved—what's more, preserved in their original state." "Rome, even though it is so expensive, dirty, and messy and it is so difficult to park, it has the most tangible spirit of history," admitted Zhu, a businessman and former Party official living in Budapest.

Enter the Tourist

Into this map of Europe steps now the Chinese tourist. In mainland China in 1990, the idea of traveling abroad was synonymous with migration. The association between the two concepts remains strong, but cultures and discourses of leisure travel are rapidly emerging. Successive liberalizations have made it much easier to obtain passports, and though the procedure is still tortuous in most cases, it is waived in the case of group package tours. In 2002, the first countries outside of Southeast Asia, Australia, and New Zealand—Germany, Egypt, Turkey, and Malta—were officially approved as destinations for such tours, followed by Cyprus and Hungary. The Approved Destination Status (ADS) meant that tourists to these countries were no longer required to masquerade as "delegations," and that the real costs of joining such tours went down. Switzerland signed a memorandum of understanding with China in November 2003, followed by the European Union in February 2004, paving the way for the expansion of ADS to most of Europe. Yet, significantly, only organized groups—no individuals—can obtain tourist visas.

International travel has been picking up rapidly. According to official statistics, 22 million PRC citizens traveled abroad in 2004, up from 16 million in 2002, 12 million in 2001, and five million in 1997. While their number is still low compared to the size of China's population—there are 11 million international travelers from much less populous Russia, for example—the latest figure is double the number of overseas travelers from Japan. The pace of the growth (20 to 30 percent annually) has led the World Tourist Organization (WTO) to estimate that in 2020, the number of Chinese tourists abroad will rise to 100 million, the highest of any country. Given that Chinese travelers are, in addition, decent spenders, a fact already blown up to mythical proportions—according to the *New York Times*, "the elusive, wealthy Chinese tourist [is] seen as the big-spending successor to the Arab tourists of the 1970's" (Brooke 2004)—the growth forecast of Chinese tourism has become a mantra for the trade. Already, tourism professionals on the receiving end are revising their standards of tourist expectations. As a German professor of tourism, speaking in Cologne at the Second European Travel Fair for the China Incoming Market, said,

The differences in cultural background, interests and behavior have to be taken into account. From the famous missing hot-water-bottle in the hotel room to the idea of providing dedicated photo spots where visitors can take pictures of themselves in front of a famous castle or telling an interesting story of former inhabitants of such a place rather than providing lengthy lectures in art history—many examples were given. (Arlt 2004)

If the WTO estimates are correct, the emergence of overseas leisure travel from China heralds potentially enormous changes in the ways societies on the receiving end perceive processes of globalization. But it is obviously no less important in both reflecting and shaping how Chinese subjects perceive their place in global hierarchies of power, modernity, and consumption. As Jennifer Craik points out, "the cultural experiences offered by tourism are consumed in terms of prior knowledge, expectations, fantasies and mythologies *generated in the tourist's origin culture rather than by the cultural offerings of the destination*" (1997:118; italics in the original). Chinese tourists go abroad with the desire for modernity, but also with the canon of scenic spots and the related cultural representations in their minds. How do tourists deal with the far less canonized meanings of sites they encounter outside of China? How will sources of authority be established over the interpretation of those sites? These questions are particularly important because of the central role of cross-border mobility in discourses of what it means to be Chinese in the modern world: indeed, one of the attractions of a trade fair in Kunming in 1999 was that visitors had their "passports" stamped as if crossing the border (Tan 2001:13).

Representations of foreign sites coming from soap operas and "new migrant" reports probably have the greatest impact on tourist expectations. This is reinforced by the fact that most travel agents and guides who put together the itineraries of and accompany Chinese tour groups are themselves recent Chinese migrants, in turn influenced by expectations toward tourist sites and guides in the Chinese domestic context. The Chinese-language Travel & Trade in Europe (Ouzhou shang-lü bao), published since the early 2000s by Wu Jingyuan, a Chinese entrepreneur in Cologne, affirms that "travel agencies or commercial service companies run by Chinese are basically responsible for the accommodation of Chinese tour and inspection groups in Europe" (Travel & Trade in Europe 2004). Since 2003, Travel & Trade in Europe has been organizing annual fairs for Chinese travel agents in Europe with the participation of Chinese embassy officials, among others. The fairs have included competitions of European Chinese tour guides (ibid.), and Wu Jingyuan has announced plans to launch a school for such guides in Cologne (Schramma 2004).

But competing representations are emerging, reflecting ideas of travel as leisure and consumption rather than the accumulation associated with "new migrants." Chinese guidebooks and travelers' atlases of foreign countries first appeared in the 1990s. A survey of some of these[2] reveals that their construction of tourist sites conforms to the scenic spot model. The spots are taken from the local tourist canon, but their hierarchy and descriptions reflect the official Chinese history-writing of the day. Much like in the early guidebooks of Shanghai, the sites are presented serendipitously and with no geographical or historical connection between them. In London, "the Greenwich meridian" and "London fog" are represented side by side with the River Thames, Buckingham Palace, and Madame Tussaud's. In Berlin, the "beautiful and sumptuous" former East German Palace of the Republic merits a description very similar to that of the Reichstag. (The Palace of the Republic, a 1980s building not even mentioned in the Michelin guide, has since been marked for demolition.) Humboldt University's importance is underlined by such historical personalities as Marx, Engels, Hegel, Einstein, and Chinese premier Zhou Enlai. The reader is told when the Berlin Wall was erected and when it was demolished, but not by whom or why. In St. Petersburg, the cruiser Aurora and the Smolny Institute, both associated with Lenin and the official Soviet history of the 1917 Bolshevik Revolution, are two of only seven sites described. Inside the Smolny, "three sacred places of the Revolution" are further identified: the congress hall, Lenin's study, and his living quarters. In Moscow, the Hotel Ukraine, a landmark Stalinist skyscraper, is compared to the Notre Dame of Paris.

Unlike Western city guidebooks, these books present no walks, neighborhoods, or atmospheric descriptions, let alone "off the beaten track" tips. On the other hand, next to the description of the sites, which occupy only one-tenth to two-thirds of the guidebooks reviewed, the books have extensive chapters devoted to the history, economy, educational system, family life, marriage customs, etiquette, festivals, gambling, and drinking habits of the countries described. Similar to the touristic representations of "minorities" in China, festivals such as the German Mardi Gras are represented as activities in which all members of the nation participate. The prominence of gambling, drinking, and erotic entertainment—not mentioned in these guidebooks but, according to Chinese guides in Berlin, a standard item on the tourist itinerary—echoes early twentieth-century representations of Shanghai.

These books, published in the late 1990s, are by now obsolete, as a series of glossier, thicker guidebooks of European countries have appeared in China's bookshops in the 2000s. The new books, and the more experienced elite travelers who use them, focus more on the "romantic" objects from the local tourist canon, such as "old towns" or wine routes. But the narratives of local Chinese tour guides in Europe continue, for now, to communicate a motley assembly of "views" that includes both objects representing modernity and places significant for the migrants' map of the city. Rather than focusing on the details of history or architecture, the guides add in entertaining stories absent from the local tourist canon. During a cruise on the Danube in Budapest for a Chinese "business delegation" in September 2001, the guide pointed out the following, in order: a casino popular with local Chinese, Castle Hill and the Chain Bridge ("symbols of Budapest"), Fishermen's Bastion, a floating restaurant, and Parliament. When talking about the Chain Bridge, the guide added a story that is absent from Hungarian tourist lore and is probably false, saying that it is also called Heroes Bridge to honor thirty workers who died when the bridge was bombed during World War II. In order to "upgrade" the Millennial Monument in Heroes Square, or perhaps simply to connect it to some familiar symbol of Western modernity, the guide referred to the angel topping its column as the Goddess of Liberty, the Chinese name commonly applied to the Statue of Liberty in New York's harbor; a guide in Berlin did the same trick with the Victory Column.

A participant in the Budapest cruise, a twenty-nine-year-old employee of a company in a township near Shanghai, did not quite know what to make of these sites: "Western and Eastern views are different. In the East, the newer the better. Here, the older the better. . . . The modern part is a bit blander, but the historical is very strong. In the last two decades, there doesn't seem to have been much development." Other tourists, however, do not hide their disappointment at the lack of "modernity" and "developed" sites, which they interpret as a lack of "tourable" places. In 2001, Zhao, a Chinese tour guide in Berlin, admitted that most of her Chinese customers are "a bit disappointed" at the lack of skyscrapers and broad avenues and find Berlin "backward" compared to Shanghai or even Hangzhou. This point is echoed by Meng, a young lecturer at one of Berlin's universities: "Here the people are so proud of the KaDeWe, the big department store. But in China, a big restaurant can be larger than that." According to Zhao, what attracts the most interest, apart from shopping and nightlife, are places associated with historical personalities, such as the Marx-Engels monument and the site of Hitler's bunker. A Russian tour guide working with Chinese tourists in St. Petersburg echoed this, saying that what her groups want to see most are the Smolny and the *Aurora*. Apparently, on a terrain where sights are yet to be canonized, tourists prefer sites for which their previous knowledge provides a sufficient set of cultural references for enshrinement.

These particular interests may be related to a particular generation of first-time travelers. But this does not mean that Chinese representations of foreign tourist sites will necessarily adopt dominant local narratives. For one thing, the Chinese state is attempting to influence these representations. Remarkably, the first large-scale study of Internet filtering in China found tourism to other countries—along with such other topics as Taiwan, Tibet, political issues, religion, and health—to be one of the topics to which the Chinese government regularly blocked Web access.[3] The various attempts to coin labels and to establish the categories according to which foreign sites should be ranked and compared to China, by migrant authors as well as by tourists, amount to attempts at wresting what Edward Said (1978:7) called "positional superiority" from the West, which has for centuries dictated those categories and defined views. Tourists and the mediators who present the attractions to them reject, or more precisely do not engage with, locally dominant representations of the localities, for example the strongly historical representation of Berlin with Nazism and Communism at its center. This lack of attention is linguistically manifested in the wanton misnaming (or renaming) of sites, often with English-sounding names—thus, the Berlin thoroughfare Unter den Linden becomes "Pipal Avenue" and the Lüneburger Heide becomes "Purple flower and sand plain" in the Germany guidebook— similar to the overwriting of Tibetan village names with Chinese names for scenic spots. But the categories that emerge in place of local representations are as yet unclear. The "development"- and modernization-centered view of the cultural, which shapes the consumption of domestic scenic spots, is evidently insufficient to deal with experiences abroad, or at least in what might be called the Western periphery: places that are neither easy-to-label "developing countries" nor the developmental paragon of North America. The Chinese tourist encounter with these sites is only beginning, and the production, dissemination, and consumption of tourist canons will be a complex process, with multiple agendas and interpretations that have the potential to impact both Chinese and non-Chinese views of being in the modern world.

One thing is certain: the Chinese state, as long as it exists in its current form, will attempt to assert its cultural authority over foreign landscapes. Early in 2004, when Chairman Hu Jintao visited Paris on the occasion of the fortieth anniversary of diplomatic relations between his state and France, the Eiffel Tower was lit with red lights, and the Champs-Elysées closed for a "dragon dance" parade. The centerpiece of further festivities—to which Nobel Prize-winning Chinese writer Gao Xingjian, who lives in Paris, was not invited—was EuroDisney, decorated in red and gold, the Chinese traditional/Communist colors. A writer with the International Herald Tribune, and probably many French people, were surprised at the "national, government-sponsored campaign" celebrating the first time that the Eiffel Tower would be lit in a single color other than its normal golden glow and the first time since the German occupation that the Champs-Elysées would be occupied by a "non-French event" (Smith 2004). But for television audiences in China, the scene was familiar and the symbolism clear. Red lights, street parades, a government-sponsored campaign—all these are the stuff of a successful tourism festival. Though a Nobel laureate, Gao Xingjian is a politically ambivalent figure almost unknown in China: the Eiffel Tower and EuroDisney, by contrast, are well-entrenched symbols of the West. For the duration of the celebrations, the vision of Into Europe's soap-opera hero was reality: Paris became a true and proper scenic spot with Chinese help.

NOTES

1   What's in a Site?

1. See, for example, a list of new publications by Lüyou Jiaoyu Chubanshe (Tourism Education Press) in *Tourism Tribune* 6, no. 1 (1991):73.

2. On the role of consumption in spiritual civilization campaigns, see Lewis (2002).

3. Mayakinfo.ru, http://www.mayakinfo.ru/news.asp?msg=10769 (accessed October 15, 2002).

4. The National Tourism Authority also publishes what it labels the number of domestic tourist trips. This figure was 240 million in 1985, 719 million in 1999, and 784 million in 2001 (Mészáros 2003). These very high figures—currently suggesting two trips for every three PRC citizens—are based on surveys of rail and road traffic (Ghimire and Li 2001:92). Therefore, although they are used by most tourism research publications, they reflect mobility in general rather than tourism specifically.

5. I am grateful to Rudolf Wagner and Catherine Yeh for acquainting me with this literature and allowing me to read a copy of Yeh's 2006 publication in manuscript.

6. On the canon of Chinese culture as represented in 1980s-1990s school textbooks, see Spakowski (1997).

7. Anagnost (1997:168) reported how, indeed, visitors to the partly newly built, partly rebuilt "old town" around the Confucian temple in Nanjing were having their photos taken at a spot on the Qinhuai River known from the seventeenth-century play *The Peach Blossom Fan*.

8. The quatrain is accessible at the PRC Foreign Ministry's Web site, http://www
.fmprc.gov.cn/chn/wjb/zzjg/ldmzs/gjlb/2033/2035/t7942.htm (accessed February 9,
2004). Substituting Cuba for the White Emperor's Citadel and South America for
Jiangling, a place in Hubei, Jiang's quatrain reads:

> Early leave from China amid coloured clouds:
> Ten thousand miles to South America we make in ten days.
> As off the shore, the storm roars madly,
> Green pines stand proud like mountains.

> 朝辞华夏彩云间
> 万里南美十日还。
> 隔岸风声狂带雨
> 青松傲骨定如山。

Li Bo's original poem 早发白帝城 reads:

> Early leave from the White Emperor's Citadel among coloured clouds:
> A thousand miles to Jiangling we make in one day.
> While on the shores the gibbons cry ceaselessly
> The lithe boat has passed ten thousand mountain folds.

> 朝辞白帝彩云间
> 千里江陵一日还。
> 两岸猿声啼不住
> 轻舟已过万重山。

The second line of the poem is itself a reference to an earlier work, the early sixth-
century *Comments to the Scripture on Waters (Shuijing zhu)* by Li Daoyuan, which says
"it is possible to set out from the White Emperor's Citadel in the morning and arrive
in Chiang-ling [Jiangling] by evening" (translation in Strassberg 1994:88). Thus, Jiang
endowed Cuba with cultural landscape references reaching back 1,500 years. I am
grateful to Xiao Putao for pointing out Jiang's quatrain.

9. Interview by Joana Breidenbach, Shanghai, 5 September 2003.

10. Writing about Chinese art music in the 1950s and '60s, Barbara Mittler (1996,
accessed 18 February 2004) describes the dominant style as "'pentatonic romanticism,'
a homophonic, virtuoso style derived from the compositional techniques of nineteenth-
century Western music writing." She goes on to say that this "invented tradition,"

which in the PRC was declared the official style of "Chinese music," "invents the death of its own folk tradition" of pitches and phraseology that do not fit the Western scale. Elsewhere, she notes that this tendency has led to the "reform" of traditional instruments, and when Chinese ensembles first began appearing in the West in 1979, listeners complained that the music they played was "not Chinese" (Mittler 1997:274–75, n. 27, 29). Thus Chinese composers were caught between divergent domestic and foreign expectations to produce "Chinese music." I thank Rudolf Wagner for introducing me to Mittler's work. For an analysis of national imagery, pentatonic phrases, and disco in a Chinese pop video clip, see Lee (2003:65–77).

11. All quotes are my translations of the Chinese text unless noted otherwise.

2   Two Sites and a Non-Site

1. On the cultural politics of the "Tibet craze" in China, see Upton (2002).

2. No or very low state funding is also typical of urban conservation, and tourism revenue is expected to but rarely does go into conservation efforts. Since gated "old towns" are often run by corporations, money earned from tickets does not necessarily flow into conservation. Lijiang has tried, but because of resistance from businesses, was unable to introduce a tourist tax prior to 2001 (Lijiang 2001).

3. Statistics from UNESCO's Man and Biosphere Reserves Web site, http://www.unesco.org/mab/sustainable/3tourism.htm (accessed January 29, 2004).

4. Ibid.

5. Zhou Yimin (International Center Manager, China Comfort Travel), in discussion with the author, Chengdu, September 10, 2003.

6. China Cultural Relics Research Association et al. 1998:432, and Miao Yuyan (Director, Marketing and Promoting Department, Sichuan Province Tourism Administration), in discussion with the author, Chengdu, September 11, 2003.

7. See the conservation report at http://whc.unesco.org/archive/repcom92.htm#637 (accessed February 9, 2004).

8. Minutes of the Sixteenth Session of the UNESCO World Heritage Committee (Santa Fe, December 7–14, 1992), http://www.unesco.org/mab/sustainable/3tourism.htm. WHC-92/CONF.002/12.

9. A recent report on Jiuzhaigou in UNESCO's World Heritage Review (Thorsell 2004)—on the benefits World Heritage status has brought to the local population—incorrectly claims that there are only twenty hotels in the service area.

10. Guo Shang, in discussion with the author, September 13, 2003.

11. See also the news item "Songpan jianshe Chuan xibei gaoyuan youke jisan zhongxin" (Songpan builds entrepot for tourists to the Northwest Sichuan highland),

from an unspecified issue of the prefectural daily *Aba Ribao*, on the government Web site of Ngawa Prefecture, http://www.aba.net.cn/abanews/tyol-aba_news_021113_01 .htm (accessed September 20, 2003).

12. On a visit to Beijing in early 2005, I learned in a discussion with Zhang Guangrui, Director of the Tourism Research Laboratory of the Chinese Academy of Social Sciences, that the project has been carried out. Ethnic song-and-dance performances are being put on at the new square. Shopkeepers have been moved into the new "Ming-Qing" houses, but Zhang predicts that they will be compelled to move out because of the high rents.

13. *Tourism Tribune* (Lüyou xuekan) is the Chinese journal of tourism research, published under supervision of the Beijing City Tourism Affairs Administration.

14. Translation by *Tourism Tribune.*

15. In discussion with the author, Chengdu, September 11, 2003.

16. The perception of uniformity is, however, mine; it is that of the Western tourist. Further empirical study will be necessary to answer the question of whether Chinese tourists themselves perceive these sites as uniform—a point raised by psychologists Janellen Huttenlocher and John Rieser—and, by extension, what the factors determining similarity are.

17. In discussion with the author, Beijing, January 26, 2005.

3   Making Sense of Scenic Spots

1. Furthermore, Mark Elvin, writing about Chinese perceptions of nature, calls Xie an advocate of "a *civilized wilderness*" for whom there was "no conflict between what we now call 'development' . . . and the spiritual inspiration to be drawn from contemplating nature" (Elvin 2004:336).

2. For an analysis of consumption as an ideal in "socialist spiritual civilization" campaigns, see Lewis (2002).

3. Data from the official Chinese Internet Information Centre, cited in http:// www.travel.ru (July 7, 2003).

4. These actions have been taken and reported within the framework of a UNESCO project to develop "models for cooperation among stakeholders" in "cultural heritage management and tourism" (http://www.unescobkk.org/culture/norad-tourism/background.htm, accessed May 15, 2004). Although the project aimed to "form mutually-beneficial alliances that will be both economically profitable and socially acceptable to local inhabitants and other stakeholders," the "Lijiang model" was developed and evaluated by the county authorities. The role and politics of UNESCO in the construction of Chinese tourism—and their differences vis-à-vis UNESCO's

involvement in, for example, Russia—raise interesting questions, but these go beyond the scope of this study. Litzinger (2004) discusses related issues in the context of The Nature Conservancy's involvement in a conservation project in Yunnan.

5. The film, a martial arts epic that heroizes the ruthless unifier of China, the Qin emperor, was shot against the background of four symbolic landscapes: an imperial compound, a mountain landscape reminiscent of a classical Chinese painting, an arid mountainous land typical of China's Mongolic-Turkic northwestern periphery, and Jiuzhaigou.

6. For a similar argument about Vietnamese tourists, see Alneng (2002:133).

7. Consider, for example, this description of Torremolinos on the Spanish coast in the 2002 edition of the popular *Guide du Routard*: "The beaches are beautiful but it is hard to see the sand: all through the summer, scores of buses disgorge the Average Joes of all countries, in flip-flops, sun hats, and T-shirts with holes" (quoted in MIT 2002:26n20. See also MIT's discussion of guidebook language there).

8. www.lvye.org/lyxz07/html/9911/abo1.htm and www.17lai.com/jingddy/SC/AB/aba_songpan.htm (accessed September 20, 2003).

9. http://www.travel.ru, September 17, 2003 (accessed September 23, 2003); see also http://www.mayakinfo.ru/news.asp?msg=9383 (accessed May 28, 2003) on a complex of log cabins with a newly built log church symbolising the traditional Russian North.

10. Sverdlovsk Province; see http://www.mayakinfo.ru/news.asp?msg=8928 (accessed April 18, 2003).

11. Karalyn Schenk of WHC, e-mail message to author, July 16 2004.

12. UNESCO's interventions had a similar dynamic in the case of Lake Baikal in Russia, although here industrial pollution rather than tourism was the main concern.

13. My argument here is similar to that made by Louisa Schein on the basis of analysing "minority" cultural performances: "The ongoing renewal of the singular authority of the modern . . . turns out to be intimately dependent on ephemeral moments of subtly nuanced cultural politics" (Schein 1999:387).

14. Apart from Barmé himself, these include Anagnost (1997), Yang (1997), Feuerwerker (1998), Hodge and Louie (1998), Lu (2002), Sun (2002), and Lee (2003).

15. Another such arena, overlapping with tourism, is the staging of "minority" culture. Indeed, my approach has much in common with Louisa Schein's endeavour to understand, through the observation of Miao cultural performances, "how the modern structure of feeling within China is repeatedly instantiated by myriad practices that are elaborated and codified in the course of various moments of sociality" (Schein 1999:363). See also Oakes 1998 and Mueggler 1999.

1. On how nationalist media discourse is shaped by a peculiar configuration of government control and market interest, see also Zhao 1998; Barmé 1999; Lynch 1999; Zhang 2001b; Donald, Keane, and Hong 2002; and Huang and Lee 2003. Cf. Lewis's (2002) analysis of how the state "sells spiritual civilization" on billboard advertising.

2. See, e.g., Jin Liangjun, ed. *Germany*, Beijing: Lüyou Jiaoyu Chubanshe, 1999; *Germany Atlas*, Beijing: China Cartographic Publishing House, 1998; Zhang Yong, ed., *Yingguo* (England), Mukden: Liaoning Jiaoyu Chubanshe, 1998; Guigui, ed., *Russia*, Canton: Guangdong Jiaoyu Chubanshe, 1997; *Eluosi Dituce* (Atlas of Russia), Beijing: Zhongguo Ditu Chubanshe, 1999; and Luo Chen, ed., *Ouzhou zhi lü*, Beijing: Guoji Wenhua Chubanshe, 1999 (two volumes of travel essays).

3. "Empirical Analysis of Internet Filtering in China," conducted by Jonathan Zittrain and Benjamin Edelman between May and November 2002, cited in Iyengar (2004).

BIBLIOGRAPHY

Alneng, Victor

    2002   "The Modern Does not Cater for Natives," *Tourist Studies* 2, no. 2:119–42.

Anagnost, Ann

    1997   *National Past-Times: Narrative, Representation, and Power in Modern China.* Durham, NC, and London: Duke University Press.

Anderson, Benedict R. O'G.

    1983   *Imagined Communities.* London: Verso.

    1998   "Nationalism, Identity, and the World-in-Motion: On the Logics of Seriality." In Pheng Cheah and Bruce Robbins, eds., *Cosmopolitics: Thinking and Feeling Beyond the Nation*, 117–33. Minneapolis: University of Minnesota Press.

Ap, John

    2003   "An Assessment of Theme Park Development in China." In Alan A. Lew, Lawrence Yu, John Ap, and Zhang Guangrui, eds., *Tourism in China*, 195–214. Binghamton, NY: Haworth Hospitality Press.

Arellano, Alexandra

    2004   "Mobility Systems and Performance at Machu Picchu." In Mimi Sheller and John Urry, eds., *Tourism Mobilities: Places to Play, Places in Play.* London and New York: Routledge.

Arlt, Wolfgang

    2004 "Into a Bright Future: Chinese Outbound Tourism to Europe Is Getting More Professional, Reliable and Tailor-Made for Special Interests." Speech presented at the Second European Travel Fair for the China Incoming Market, Cologne, January 3–4. Reprinted in *Travel & Trade in Europe*, no. 1–2:15.

Baikaltur

    2004 *Mezhdunarodnaia turisticheskaia vystavka "Baikaltur"* (Baikaltur International Tourism Fair). Official catalogue. Irkutsk: SibEkspoTsentr.

Barmé, Geremie

    1999 *In the Red*. New York: Columbia University Press.

Becker, Jasper

    2004 "Faking it: Chinese Burn Their Bridges with the Past." *The Independent*, April 2, 20–21.

Boyer, Marc

    1999 *Le tourisme de l'an 2000*. Lyon: Presses Universitaires de Lyon.

Brook, Timothy

    1998 *The Confusions of Pleasure: Commerce and Culture in Ming China*. Berkeley, Los Angeles, and London: University of California Press.

Brooke, James

    2004 "In the Pacific, Vying for Elusive Prey: China's Rich Tourists." *The New York Times*, May 24.

Buck, Roy C.

    1977 "The Ubiquitous Tourist Brochure: Explorations in Its Intended and Unintended Use." *Annals of Tourism Research* 4, no. 4: 195–207.

Butcher, Jim

    2003 *The Moralization of Tourism*. London and New York: Routledge.

Buzard, James

    1993 *The Beaten Track: European Tourism, Literature and the Ways to Culture, 1800–1918*. New York: Oxford University Press.

Cahill, James

    1992 "Huang Shan Paintings as Pilgrimage Pictures." In Susan Naquin and Chün-Fang Yü, eds., *Pilgrims and Sacred Sites in China*, 246–92. Berkeley, Los Angeles, and London: University of California Press.

Cater, E[rlan]

    2001 "Ecotourism." In Neil J. Smelser and Paul B. Baltes, eds., *International Encyclopedia of the Social & Behavioral Sciences*, 4165–68. Amsterdam and New York: Elsevier.

Chen, Nancy N., Constance D. Clark, Suzanne Z. Gottschang, and Lyn Jeffery
  2001   *China Urban: Ethnographies of Contemporary Culture*. Durham, NC and
         London: Duke University Press.
China Cultural Relics Research Association, China Scenic Areas Association,
    China Tourism Association, China Museum Research Association, and China
    Map Press (Zhongguo Wenwu Xuehui, Zhongguo Fengjing Minshengqu
    Xiehui, Zhongguo Lüyou Xiehui, Zhongguo Bowuguan Xuehui, and Zhongguo
    Ditu Chubanshe), eds.
  1998   *Zhongguo zhuming fengjing mingsheng lüyou daguan* (Tourist Encyclopedia
         of China's Famous Scenic Areas). Beijing: Zhongguo Ditu Chubanshe.
Cohen, Erik
  1985   "The Tourist Guide: The Origins, Structure and Dynamics of a Role."
         Annals of Tourism Research 12:5–29.
Craik, Jennifer
  1997   "The Culture of Tourism." In Chris Rojek and John Urry, eds., *Touring
         Cultures: Transformations of Travel and Theory*, 113–36. London and New
         York: Routledge.
Davis, Deborah S.
  1999   *The Consumer Revolution in Urban China*. Berkeley, Los Angeles, and
         London: University of California Press.
Diller + Scofidio
  1994   "Suitcase Studies: The Production of a National Past." In *Back to the Front:
         Tourisms of War*, 32–108. Caen: F.R.A.C. Basse-Normandie.
Donald, Stephanie Hemelryk, Michael Keane, and Yin Hong, eds.
  2002   *Made in China: Consumption, Content and Crisis*. London and New York:
         RoutledgeCurzon.
Dott, Brian R.
  2002   Signifying Mount Tai: Modern Meanings of an Ancient Site. Paper pre-
         sented at the Asian Studies Annual Meeting, Washington, D.C.
Duang Songting
  2000   *A Heritage Protection and Tourism Development Case Study of Lijiang Ancient
         Town, China*. Report submitted to UNESCO Office of the Regional
         Advisor for Culture in Asia and the Pacific, Bhaktapur, Nepal.
         http://www.unescobkk.org/culture/archives/lijiang-2.pdf (accessed
         February 17, 2004).
Duara, Prasenjit
  1997   "Nationalists among Transnationals: Overseas Chinese and the Idea of
         China, 1900–1911." In Aihwa Ong and Donald Nonini, eds., *Ungrounded*

Empires: The Cultural Politics of Modern Chinese Transnationalism, 39–60.
London and New York: Routledge.

Edensor, Tim

1998   Tourists at the Taj: Performance and Meaning at a Symbolic Site. London and
        New York: Routledge.

2001   "Performing Tourism, Staging Tourism." Tourist Studies 1, no. 1:59–81.

2002   National Identity, Popular Culture and Everyday Life. Oxford and New York:
        Berg.

Elvin, Mark

2004   The Retreat of the Elephants: An Environmental History of China. New Haven:
        Yale University Press.

Ely, Christopher

2003   "The Origins of Russian Scenery: Volga River Tourism and Russian
        Landscape Aesthetics." Slavic Review 62, no. 4:666–82.

Farquhar, Judith

2002   Appetites: Food and Sex in Postsocialist China. Durham, NC and London:
        Duke University Press.

Farrer, James

2002   Opening Up: Youth Sex Culture and Market Reform in Shanghai. Chicago:
        University of Chicago Press.

Feuerwerker, Yi-tsi Mei

1998   Ideology, Power, Text: Self-Representation and the Peasant "Other" in Modern
        Chinese Literature. Stanford: Stanford University Press.

Friman, H. Richard

2002   "Evading the Divine Wind Through the Side Door: The Transformation
        of Chinese Migration to Japan." In Pál Nyíri and Igor R. Saveliev, eds.,
        Globalising Chinese Migration, 9–34. Aldershot, Hampshire: Ashgate.

Ghimire, Krishna B., and Zhou Li

2001   "The Economic Role of National Tourism in China." In Krishna B.
        Ghimire, ed., The Native Tourist, 86–108. London and Sterling, VA:
        Earthscan.

Gladney, Dru

1994   "Representing Nationality in China: Refiguring Majority/Minority
        Identities." Journal of Asian Studies 53, no. 1:92–123.

2002   "Alterity Motives." In Pál Nyíri and Joana Breidenbach, eds., China
        Inside Out. http://cio.ceu.hu/courses/CIO/modules/Moduleo7Gladney/
        Gladney_02.html.

Gorsuch, Anne E.

    2003 "'There's No Place Like Home': Soviet Tourism in Late Stalinism." *Slavic Review* 62, no. 4:760–85.

Gu Guanying

    1922 *Zhonghua quanguo mingsheng guji daguan.* Shanghai: Dalu Tushu Gongsi.

Harvey, David

    1989 *The Condition of Postmodernity: An Enquiry into the Origins of Cultural Change.* Cambridge, MA: Basil Blackwell.

Hashimoto, A.

    2000 "Environmental Perception and Sense of Responsibility of the Tourism Industry in Mainland China, Taiwan, and Japan." *Journal of Sustainable Tourism* 8, no. 2:131–46.

Hirsch, Francine

    2003 "Getting to Know 'The Peoples of the USSR': Ethnographic Exhibits as Soviet Virtual Tourism, 1923–1934." *Slavic Review* 62, no. 4:683–709.

Hodge, Bob, and Kam Louie

    1998 *The Politics of Chinese Language and Culture: The Art of Reading Dragons.* London and New York: Routledge.

Huang, Yu, and Chin-Chuan Lee

    2003 "Peddling Party Ideology for a Profit: Media and the Rise of Chinese Nationalism in the 1990s." In Gary D. and Ming-Yeh T. Rawnsley, eds., *Political Communications in Greater China*, 41–61. London and New York: RoutledgeCurzon.

Huang Fengjia

    1884 Introduction to *Shenjiang shengjingtu.* Shanghai: Shenbaoguan and Shenchang Shuhuashi.

Hyde, Sandra Theresa

    2001 "Sex Tourism Practices on the Periphery: Eroticizing Ethnicity and Pathologizing Sex on the Lancang." In Chen et al., eds., *China Urban: Ethnographies of Contemporary Culture*, 143–64. Durham, NC and London: Duke University Press.

Ivy, Marilyn

    1995 *Discourses of the Vanishing.* Chicago: University of Chicago Press.

Iyengar, Jayanthi

    2004 "Digital China is Booming." *Asia Times Online*, February 18.

http://www.atimes.com/atimes/China/FB18Ad01.html (accessed
February 18, 2004).

Jing Ziyu

    1991   "Renzhen zongjie lüyouye fazhan di jiben jingyan" (Earnestly sum up
the fundamental experience of tourism development). *Tourism Tribune*
(Beijing) 6, no. 1:2–3.

Ju Yuhua

    2004   "Xin yimin zinü jiaoyu xianzhuang ji duice yanjiu" (The educational situ-
ation of new migrants' children and policy responses). Paper presented
at the fifth conference of the International Society for the Study of Chinese Overseas, Elsinore, Denmark, May 10–14.

Koenker, Diane P.

    2003   "Travel to Work, Travel to Play: On Russian Tourism, Travel, and Lei-
sure." *Slavic Review* 62, no. 4:658–65.

Koshar, Rudy

    2000   *German Travel Cultures*. Oxford and New York: Berg.

    2002   "Seeing, Traveling, and Consuming." In Rudy Koshar, ed., *Histories of
Leisure*, 1–24. Oxford and New York: Berg.

Lee, Gregory B.

    2003   *Chinas Unlimited: Making the Imaginaries of China and Chineseness*. London
and New York: Routledge.

Lewis, Steven Wayne

    2002   "What Can I Do for Shanghai? Selling Spiritual Civilization in China's
Cities." In Stephanie Hemelryk Donald, Michael Keane, and Yin Hong,
eds., *Made in China: Consumption, Content and Crisis*, 139–151. London and
New York: RoutledgeCurzon.

Li Feng

    1982   "Zai Hai Rui mu" (At Hai Rui's tomb). *Tourist* (Beijing), no. 2:13.

Li Hairui

    1991   "'Dianzi hangye'" (The "site business"). *Tourism Tribune* (Beijing) 6,
no. 2:1.

Li Wenfang

    1987   *Zhongguo mingsheng suoyin*. Beijing: Zhongguo Lüyou Chubanshe.

Li Yiping

    2003   "Development of the Nanshan Cultural Tourism Zone in Hainan, China:
Achievements Made and Issues to be Resolved." *Tourism Geographies* 5,
no. 4:436–45.

Liao Rongrong

2003   *Zhongguo shi jia daoyou.* 2 vols. Chengdu: Sichuan Daxue Chubanshe.

Lijiang

2001   *Report on the Implementation of the Action Plan of Lijiang, China.* Submitted
to the UNESCO Conference/Workshop on "Culture Heritage Manage-
ment and Tourism: Models for Cooperation among Stakeholders,"
Lijiang, October 8–18. http://www.unescobkk.org/culture/archives/
5.pdf.

Lim, Louisa

2004   "China Tourist Town's Culture Clash." *BBC News,* June 28. http://news.bbc
.co.uk/go/pr/fr/-/1/hi/world/asia-pacific/3839443.stm.

Lin Sheng'r

2002a   "Nü beibao du chuang Yindu" (Female backpacker, alone, hits India).
Travel Times (Shanghai), July 11, A3.

2002b   "Zhen xiwang lai shi zuo yi zhi niao" (I really hope to be reborn as a
bird), *Travel Times* (Shanghai), July 11, A3.

Lindberg, Kreg, Clem Tisdell, and Dayuan Xue

2003   "Ecotourism in China's Nature Reserves." In Alan A. Lew, Lawrence
Yu, John Ap, and Zhang Guangrui, eds., *Tourism in China,* 103–25. Bing-
hamton, NY: Haworth Hospitality Press.

Litzinger, Ralph

2004   "The Mobilization of 'Nature:' Perspectives from Northwest Yunnan."
China Quarterly 178:488–505.

Liu, Xin

1997   "Space, Mobility, and Flexibility: Chinese Villagers and Scholars
Negotiate Power at Home and Abroad." In Aihwa Ong and Donald
Nonini, eds., *Ungrounded Empires: The Cultural Politics of Modern Chinese
Transnationalism,* 91–114. London and New York: Routledge.

Löfgren, Orvar

1999   *On Holiday. A History of Vacationing.* Berkeley, Los Angeles, and London:
University of California Press.

Lomanov, Alexander V.

2002   "On the Periphery of the 'Clash of Civilisations': Discourse and Geo-
politics in Russian-Chinese Relations." In Pál Nyíri and Joana Breidenbach, eds., *China Inside Out: Contemporary Chinese Nationalism and
Transnationalism.* http://cio.ceu.hu. Paper edition: Budapest: Central
European University Press, 2005.

Lu, Sheldon H.

    2002   *China, Transnational Visuality, Global Postmodernity*. Stanford: Stanford University Press.

Lynch, David

    1999   *After the Propaganda State: Media, Politics, and "Thought Work" in Reformed China*. Stanford: Stanford University Press.

MacCannell, Dean

    1976   *The Tourist: A New Theory of the Leisure Class*. New York: Schocken.

    2001   "Tourist Agency." *Tourist Studies* 1, no. 1:23–37.

McReynolds, Louise

    2003   *Russia at Play*. Ithaca, NY and London: Cornell University Press.

Mandler, Peter

    1999   "'The Wand of Fancy': The Historical Imagination of the Victorian Tourist." In Marius Kwint, Christopher Breward, and Jeremy Aynsley, eds., *Material Memories: Design and Evocation*, 125–42. Oxford and New York: Berg.

Mayhew, Bradley

    2004   *Lonely Planet Shanghai*. 2nd ed. Footscray, Victoria, Australia: Lonely Planet Publications.

Mészáros, Klára

    2003   "Turizmus—jönnek a kínaiak" (Tourism—the Chinese are coming). *Vélemények, Kommentárok, Információk* (newsletter of the Institute for World Economics, Hungarian Academy of Sciences), no. 51 (February 20).

Miller, Daniel

    1994   *Modernity: An Ethnographic Approach: Dualism and Mass Consumption in Trinidad*. Oxford and New York: Berg.

MIT (équipe)

    2002   *Tourismes 1: Lieux communs*. Paris: Belin.

Mittler, Barbara

    1996   "Chinese New Music as a Politicized Language: Orthodox Melodies as Dangerous Tunes." Indiana East Asian Working Paper Series on Language and Politics in Modern China. http://www.indiana.edu/~easc/resources/working_paper/noframe_10a_chin.htm (accessed May 15, 2004).

    1997   *Dangerous Tunes: The Politics of Chinese Music in Hong Kong, Taiwan, and the People's Republic of China since 1949*. Wiesbaden: Harrassowitz.

Moeran, Brian

    1983   "The Language of Japanese Tourism." *Annals of Tourism Research* 10, no. 1:93–108.

Mueggler, Erik

    2002   "Dancing Fools: Politics of Culture and Place in a 'Traditional Nationality Festival,'" *Modern China* 28, no. 1:3–38.

Nader, Laura

    1997   "Controlling Processes: Tracing the Dynamic Components of Power." *Current Anthropology* 38, no. 5:711–37.

Naquin, Susan, and Chün-Fang Yü, eds.

    1992   *Pilgrims and Sacred Sites in China*. Berkeley, Los Angeles, and London: University of California Press.

National Tourism Administration International Market Development Department Propaganda Promotion Office (Guojia Lüyouju Guoji Shichang Kaifasi Xuanchuan Cujinchu)

    1991   "90 Zhongguo lüyouye di huigu yu qianzhan." *Tourism Tribune* (Beijing) 6, no. 1:1.

Nyíri, Pál

    2001   "Expatriating is Patriotic? The Discourse on 'New Migrants' in the People's Republic of China and Identity Construction among Recent Migrants from the PRC." *Journal of Ethnic and Migration Studies* 27, no. 4: 635–53.

    2002a   "Mobility, Entrepreneurship, and Sex: How Narratives of Modernity Help Chinese Women in Hungary Evade Gender Constraints." In Pál Nyíri and Igor R. Saveliev, eds., *Globalising Chinese Migration*, 290–308. Aldershot, Hampshire: Ashgate.

    2002b   "The 'New Migrant': State and Market Constructions of Modernity and Patriotism." In Pál Nyíri and Joana Breidenbach, eds., *China Inside Out: Contemporary Chinese Nationalism and Transnationalism*. http://cio.ceu.hu. Paper edition: Budapest: Central European University Press, 2005.

    2002c   "Chinese in Hungary and their Significant Others: A Multi-Sited Approach to Transnational Practice and Discourse." *Identities* 9, no. 1:69–86.

    2005   "Global Modernizers or Local Subalterns? Parallel Perceptions of Chinese Transnationals in Hungary." *Journal of Ethnic and Migration Studies* 31(4):659–74.

Oakes, Tim

    1998   *Tourism and Modernity in China*. London and New York: Routledge.

Ong, Aihwa

    1997   "Chinese Modernities: Narratives of Nation and of Capitalism." In Aihwa Ong and Donald M. Nonini, eds., *Ungrounded Empires*, 171–202. London and New York: Routledge.

Ousby, Ian

    1990   *The Englishman's England: Taste, Travel and the Rise of Tourism*. Cambridge: Cambridge University Press.

Palmowski, Jan

    2002   "Travels with Baedeker—The Guidebook and the Middle Classes in Victorian and Edwardian Britain." In Rudy Koshar, ed., *Histories of Leisure*, 105–30. Oxford and New York: Berg.

Parker, David

    2003   "Is There a British Chinese Public Sphere?" In Gary D. and Ming-Yeh T. Rawnsley, eds., *Political Communications in Greater China*, 239–60. London and New York: RoutledgeCurzon.

Peters, Heather

    2001   "Making Tourism Work for Heritage Preservation: Lijiang—A Case Study." In Tan Chee-Beng, Sydney C. H. Cheung, and Yang Hui, eds., *Tourism, Anthropology and China*, 313–32. Bangkok: White Lotus Press.

Petersen, Ying Yang

    1995   "The Chinese Landscape as a Tourist Attraction: Image and Reality." In Alan A. Lew and Lawrence Yu, eds., *Tourism in China*, 141–54. Boulder, San Francisco, and Oxford: Westview Press.

Picard, Michel

    1993   "Cultural Tourism in Bali: National Integration and Regional Differentiation." In M. Hitchcock, V. King, and M. Parnwell, eds., *Tourism in South-East Asia*, 71–98. London and New York: Routledge.

Qian Wei

    2003   "Travel Agencies in China at the Turn of the Millennium." In Alan A. Lew, Lawrence Yu, John Ap, and Zhang Guangrui, eds., *Tourism in China*, 143–64. Binghamton, NY: Haworth Hospitality Press.

Qiao Yu

    2001   "Construction of 'Big Museum': a New Thought about the Future Development of Badaling Great Wall Scenic Spot." *Tourism Tribune* (Beijing) 3:41–43.

Rea, Michael H.

    2000   "A *Furusato* Away from Home." *Annals of Tourism Research* 27, no. 3:638–60.

Rofel, Lisa

    1992   "Rethinking Modernity: Space and Factory Discipline in China." *Cultural Anthropology* 7, no. 1:93–114.

Rojek, Chris

    1997   "Indexing, Dragging and the Social Construction of Tourist Sights." In Chris Rojek and John Urry, eds., *Touring Cultures: Transformations of Travel and Theory*, 52–74. London and New York: Routledge.

Rojek, Chris, and John Urry, eds.

    1997   *Touring Cultures: Transformations of Travel and Theory.* London and New York: Routledge.

Said, Edward

    1978   *Orientalism.* New York: Pantheon Books.

Sandomirskaya, Irina

    1998   "Proletarian Tourism: Incorporated History and Incorporated Rhetoric." In Mette Bryld and Erik Kulavig, eds., *Soviet Civilization Between Past and Present*, 39–52. Odense: Odense University Press.

Schein, Louisa

    1997   "Gender and Internal Orientalism in China." *Modern China* 23, no. 1:69–98.

    1999   "Performing Modernity." *Cultural Anthropology* 14, no. 3:361–95.

Schramma, Fritz

    2004   Speech by the Head Mayor of Cologne at the Second Annual Chinese Travel Fair in Europe. *Travel & Trade in Europe*, no. 1–2:1.

Shaanxi Shifan Daxue Chubanshe

    2003   *Zhongguo tubu chuanyue* (Traversing China on foot; English title: *A Guide for Chinese Hikers*). Taiyuan.

Shandong Youyi Shushi

    1988   *Lüyou xiaobaike* (Pocket tourism encyclopedia). Jinan.

Shtyurmer, Yu. A.

    1985   *Kratkii spravochnik turista.* 3rd ed. Moscow: Profizdat.

Sichuan Province Local Gazetteers Editorial Committee (Sichuan Sheng Difangzhi Bianzuan Weiyuanhui)

    1996   *Emeishan zhi* (A gazetteer of Mount Emei). Chengdu: Sichuan Kexue Jishu Chubanshe.

Sichuan Province Tourism Administration and Sichuan Province Tourism Association, eds.

    2002   *Sichuan daoyouci jingxuan.* Beijing: Zhongguo Lüyou Chubanshe.

Smith, Craig S.

    2004 "Paris Fêtes China with Red Eiffel Tower and Fanfare." *International Herald Tribune*, January 26, 3.

Sofield, Trevor H. B., and Fung Mei Sarah Li

    1998 "Tourism Development and Cultural Policies in China." *Annals of Tourism Research* 25, no. 2:362–92.

Songpan xianzhi (Songpan county gazetteer)

    [1924] 1967 Taipei: Taiwan Xuesheng Chubanshe.

Spakowski, Nicola

    1997 *Helden, Monumente, Traditionen. Nationale Identität und historisches Bewusstsein in der VR China.* Münster: LIT.

Stanley, Nick

    1998 *Being Ourselves for You: The Global Display of Cultures.* London: Middlesex University Press.

Strassberg, Richard E.

    1994 *Inscribed Landscapes: Travel Writing from Imperial China.* Berkeley, Los Angeles, and London: University of California Press.

Sun, Wanning

    2002 *Leaving China: Media, Migration, and the Transnational Imagination.* Lanham, Boulder, New York, and Oxford: Rowman & Littlefield.

Swain, Margaret Byrne

    2001 "Cosmopolitan Tourism and Minority Politics in the Stone Forest." In Tan Chee-Beng, Sydney C. H. Cheung, and Yang Hui, eds., *Tourism, Anthropology and China*, 125–46. Bangkok: White Lotus Press.

Tan Chee-Beng, Sydney C. H. Cheung, and Yang Hui, eds.

    2001 *Tourism, Anthropology and China.* Bangkok: White Lotus Press.

Tang Zuoxin

    1982 "Guilin shan shui jia tianxia" (Guilin's mountains and waters have no match under heaven). *Tourist* (Beijing), no. 4: 21.

Teng Xincai

    2001 "On Tourist Culture in the Mid- and Late Ming Dynasty." *Tourism Tribune* (Beijing), no. 6:64–69.

Thorsell, Jim

    2004 "The Natural World Heritage of China." *World Heritage Review* 36.

Tian, Chengke

    1981 *Pictures and Poems of Mount Emei's Ten Sceneries* (Emei shi jing tu shi). Beijing: Qinggong Chubanshe.

TIN (Tibet Information Network)

2002 "'Rebuilding' and 'Renovation' in Lhasa." Special report. www.tibetinfo
.net/news-updates/2002/1009.htm (accessed March 4, 2004).

Tourism Tribune (Lüyou xuekan)

2001 "Cheng xu er shang, tansuo lüyou qiye jituanhua jingying fazhan zhi
lu" (Grasp the opportunity to soar: study the road of corporatizing the
tourism business), no. 1:12–16. Beijing.

Tourist (Lüyou)

1982 "Su Dongpo zai di-er guxiang" (Su Shi in his second home), no. 2:14–
15. Beijing.

Travel & Trade in Europe (Ouzhou shang-lü bao)

2004 "Ouzhou huaren lüyou nianhui wanmei luomu" (Annual Chinese travel
fair in Europe a resounding success), no. 1–2:1. Cologne.

Travel Times (Lüyou shibao)

2002 "Shanghai: jing guan qi bian" (Shanghai: quietly watching its changes).
July 11:D1. Shanghai.

Upton, Janet L.

2002 "The Politics and Poetics of Sister Drum." In Timothy J. Craig and Richard
King, eds., Global Goes Local: Popular Culture in Asia, 99–119. Vancouver and
Toronto: UBC Press.

Urry, John

1990 The Tourist Gaze. London, Newbury Park, and New Delhi: Sage.

Usyskin, Grigorii

2000 Ocherki istorii rossiiskogo turizma (Essays on the history of Russian
tourism). St. Petersburg: Gerda.

Wagner, Rudolf G.

1992 "Reading the Chairman Mao Memorial Hall in Beijing: The Tribulations
of the Implied Pilgrim." In Susan Naquin and Chün-Fang Yü, eds., Pilgrims and Sacred Sites in China, 378–423. Berkeley, Los Angeles, and London:
University of California Press.

Walsh, Eileen R.

2001 "Living with the Myth of Matriarchy: the Mosuo and Tourism." In Tan
Chee-Beng, Sydney C. H. Cheung, and Yang Hui, eds., Tourism, Anthropology and China, 93–124. Bangkok: White Lotus Press.

Walsh, E. R., and M. B. Swain

2004 "Creating Modernity by Touring Paradise: Domestic Ethnic Tourism in
Yunnan, China." Tourism Recreation Research, 29(2):59–68.

Wang Chunwu

    1982   "Deng mingshan, ting chuanqi, guan meijin—Qingcheng lansheng."
          Tourist (Beijing), no. 1:26–27.

Wang, Jing

    2001   "The State Question in Chinese Popular Cultural Studies." *Inter-Asia
          Cultural Studies* 2, no. 1:35–52.

Watson, James L.

    1985   "Standardizing the Gods: The Promotion of T'ien Hou ("Empress of
          Heaven") Along the South China Coast, 960–1960." In David Johnson,
          Andrew J. Nathan, and Evelyn S. Rawski, eds., *Popular Culture in Late
          Imperial China*, 292–324. Berkeley, Los Angeles, and London: University
          of California Press.

    1992   "The Renegotiation of Chinese Cultural Identity in the Post-Mao Era."
          In Jeffrey N. Wasserstrom and Elizabeth J. Perry, eds., *Popular Protest
          and Political Culture in Modern China*, 67–84. Boulder, San Francisco,
          and Oxford: Westview Press.

Wei Xiaoan, Liu Zhaoping, and Zhang Shumin

    1999   *Zhongguo lüyouye xin shiji fazhan da qushi* (Trends in China's tourism
          development in the new century). Guangzhou: Guangdong Lüyou
          Chubanshe.

Williams, Allan M., and C. Michael Hall, eds.

    2000   *Tourism and Migration*. Special issue, *Tourism Geographies* 2, no. 1.

Williams, Raymond

    1961   *The Long Revolution*. London: Chatto and Windus.

World Heritage Center

    2001   Report on the State of Conservation of World Heritage Sites.
          http://whc.unesco.org

World Heritage Committee

    2002   "Report on the state of conservation of the Historic Sanctuary of Machu
          Picchu (Peru): Report of the UNESCO-IUCN-ICOMOS Mission to
          Machu Picchu, Peru, February 25 to March 1, 2002." WHC-02/CONF
          .202/INF.10. http://whc.unesco.org

Wu, Pei-yi

    1992   "An Ambivalent Pilgrim to T'ai Shan in the Seventeenth Century." In
          Susan Naquin and Chün-Fang Yü, eds., *Pilgrims and Sacred Sites in China*,
          65–88. Berkeley, Los Angeles, and London: University of California
          Press.

Xiang Dawan

    1982   "Buermen, Guanyinyan, Bazhentu" (No Second Gate, Avalokitesvara Rock, Eight Columns Picture). *Tourist* (Beijing), no. 4: 32–33.

Xiao, Honggen

    2003   "Leisure in China." In Alan A. Lew, Lawrence Yu, John Ap, and Zhang Guangrui, eds., *Tourism in China*, 263–75. Binghamton, NY: Haworth Hospitality Press.

Xiao Jing and A Hua

    1992   *Zhongguo mingsheng fengguang shi ci xuan* (Selected landscape poetry on China's scenic sites). Beijing: Zhongguo Shudian.

Xiao Tihui

    1991   "Wo guo lüyouye di chanpin fansi ji qi zhanlüe" (Product thinking in our country's tourism business). *Tourism Tribune* (Beijing) 6, no. 2:7–13.

Xu, Gang

    1999   *Tourism and Local Economic Development in China*. Richmond, Surrey: Curzon.

Xu Xinjian

    2001   "Developing China: Influence of 'Ethnic Tourism' and 'Ethnic Tourees.'" In Tan Chee-Beng, Sydney C. H. Cheung, and Yang Hui, eds., *Tourism, Anthropology, and China*, 193–214. Bangkok: White Lotus Press.

Yamashita, Shinji

    2003   *Bali and Beyond*. Oxford: Berghahn.

Yang, Mayfair Mei-hui

    1997   "Mass Media and Transnational Subjectivity in Shanghai: Notes on (Re)cosmopolitanism in a Chinese Metropolis." In Aihwa Ong and Donald M. Nonini, eds., *Ungrounded Empires*, 287–322. London and New York: Routledge.

Yeh, Catherine Vance

    2002   "Representing the City: Shanghai and Its Maps." In David Faure and Tao Tao Liu, eds., *Town and Country in China: Identity and Perception*, 167–202. New York: Palgrave.

    2006   *Shanghai Love: Courtesans, Intellectuals, and Entertainment Culture, 1850–1910*. Seattle and London: University of Washington Press.

Yinguang

    1934   *Emeishan zhi* (A gazetteer of Mount Emei). Shanghai: Guoguang Yinshuju.

Ying Shilin, ed.

    1992   *Ai zuguo di gushi* (Patriotic stories). Beijing.

Yizhi

    2002   *Zang di niupi shu*. Beijing: Zhongguo Qingnian Chubanshe.

Yong Xiaoru, ed.

    1999   *Zhongguo mingsheng gailan*. Beijing: Zhongguo Renshi Chubanshe.

Yu, Pauline

    1989   *The Reading of Imagery in the Chinese Poetic Tradition*. Princeton, NJ:
                Princeton University Press.

Yu Xuecai

    1991   "Zhongguo Lüyou Wenxue Yanjiuhui di-si jie nianhui xueshu lunwen
                zongshu" (A review of scholarly papers at the China Travel Literature
                Research Association's fourth annual meeting). *Tourism Tribune* (Beijing)
                6, no. 1:59–60.

Zhang Dalin

    1982   "Shi jing, shi hua" (Land of poems, words of verse). *Tourist* (Beijing) no.
                4:22–23.

Zhang Guangrui

    2003   "China's Tourism Since 1978 : Policies, Experiences, and Lessons
                Learned." In Alan A. Lew, Lawrence Yu, John Ap, and Zhang Guang-
                rui, eds., *Tourism in China*, 13–34. Binghamton, NY: Haworth Hospi-
                tality Press.

Zhang, Xudong

    2001a "The Making of the Post-Tiananmen Intellectual Field: A Critical
                Overview." In Zhang Xudong, *Whither China?*, 1–78. Durham, NC and
                London: Duke University Press.

    2001b "Nationalism, Mass Culture, and Intellectual Strategies in Post-
                Tiananmen China." In Zhang Xudong, ed., *Whither China?*, 315–48.
                Durham, NC and London: Duke University Press.

Zhang Yongxian

    1991   "Qianghua chanye yishi, wanshan chanpin jigou" (Strengthen profes-
                sionalism, optimize product structure). *Tourism Tribune* (Beijing) 6, no.
                1:29–31.

Zhao, Yuezhi

    1998   *Media, Market, and Democracy in China: Between the Party Line and the Bottom
                Line*. Urbana: University of Illinois Press.

INDEX

LIBRARY OF CONGRESS
CATALOGING-IN-PUBLICATION DATA

Nyíri, Pál.
Scenic spots : Chinese tourism, the state,
and cultural authority / Pál Nyíri.
p. cm.
"A China program book."
Includes bibliographical references and index.
ISBN 0-295-98588-7 (hbk. : alk. paper)
ISBN 0-295-98589-5 (pbk. : alk. paper)
1. Tourism—China.   I. Title.
G155.C55N95 2005   338.4'79151—dc22
2005026735

PÁL NYÍRI is Lecturer in the department of anthropology and Director of the Program in Applied Anthropology, Macquarie University, Sidney, Australia. His current research focuses primarily on the issue of cultural authority in the context of increasing population mobility in China.